PRAISE FOR *EACH DAY A RENEWED BEGINNING*

"An important reminder of the simple truths which can bring us to a peaceful mind and heart."

—Becca Anderson, author of *Prayers for Calm*

"Karen Casey is a wise woman, writing more than twenty books based on her own experiences, including her long-time spiritual practices with the 12 steps and *A Course in Miracles*. Her writing and her speaking have affected millions of lives. As she became older, she shared with us her own trials and stresses and offered ways to stay centered in the present. As the world seemed to become crazier and crazier, she offered a still place to breathe and make good decisions about what we could control and how we can do it."

—Jan Johnson, Publisher Emerita Conari Press

Each Day
a Renewed
Beginning

Each Day
a Renewed
Beginning

Meditations for a Peaceful Journey

KAREN CASEY

Conari
Press

CORAL GABLES

Published by Conari Press an imprint of Mango Publishing Group, a division of Mango Media Inc.

Cover Design: Gabrielle Mechaber
Layout & Design: Morgane Leoni
Cover Photo: © wittybear / Adobe Stock
Interior Flowers Illustrations: © airmel / Adobe Stock

For permission requests, please contact the publisher at:

Mango Publishing Group
2850 S Douglas Road, 2nd Floor
Coral Gables, FL 33134 USA
info@mango.bz

For special orders, quantity sales, course adoptions and corporate sales, please email the publisher at sales@mango.bz. For trade and wholesale sales, please contact Ingram Publisher Services at: customer.
service@ingramcontent.com
or +1.800.509.4887.

Each Day a Renewed Beginning: Meditations for a Peaceful Journey

Library of Congress Cataloging-in-Publication number: 2021934476
ISBN: (p) 978-1-64250-566-5, (e) 978-1-64250-567-2
BISAC category code PHI023000, PHILOSOPHY / Taoist

Printed in the United States of America

CONTENTS

FOREWORD

There is a saying attributed to many different people that the days go slow and the years go fast. That may well be true, and sometimes it might be the other way around. But the real truth is that in recovery, in living each day, even each hour, there is no time but the present time. And there is no one who is responsible for how we live those days and hours except ourselves.

Many years ago, Karen Casey wrote a book called *Each Day a New Beginning*. That book has helped thousands, maybe millions, of people since. It's a book to turn to every day—when we're trying to live in the present, trying to deal with our daily lives without creating blame, drama, or more stress. One of the first daily meditation books of its kind, it has become a classic.

I first met Karen shortly after *Each Day a New Beginning* was published. We became work friends, as the line of books she was publishing (and for some of them, also writing) was being copublished by the publisher where I was the editorial director. Every time I spoke with Karen in those early days, I felt more centered and grounded. And so often I took away a practical piece of wisdom or a small practice that improved my daily life.

Karen Casey is a wise woman who has written more than twenty books based on her own experiences, including her long-time spiritual practices with the 12 steps and *A Course in Miracles*. Her writing and her speaking have affected millions of lives. As she became older, she shared with us her own trials and stresses and offered ways to stay centered in the present. As the world seemed to become crazier and crazier, she offered a still place to breathe and make good decisions about what we could control and how we can do it.

When I was the publisher at Conari Press, I was privileged with the opportunity to edit and publish several of Karen's books, including *All We Have Is, All We Need*—even that title makes me pay attention. Or *Change Your Mind and Your Life Will Follow*, what a concept!

Karen Casey has been one of the wise women of my life, and with *Each Day a Renewed Beginning*, she continues in that role for me and I trust for you—for all of us who value a simple and profound daily practice that can bring us sanity and peace, teach us our own worth, and help us go out into the world to make it a better place in myriad daily ways. Most of all, her words teach us to live in the moment of our days, whatever they may bring.

—JAN JOHNSON,
Publisher Emerita, Conari Press

INTRODUCTION

What a thrill it is to be greeting you from the pages of another meditation book, one of a dozen meditation books I have written since I walked through the doors of Alcoholics Anonymous in 1976. My first daily book, *Each Day a New Beginning*, was for women in 12-step recovery. It was penned in 1981; over the intervening years, I have written several additional books dealing with myriad life struggles, and I have had many. But the meditation genre called to me again in 2020 in this time of Covid. My own quarantine became the perfect opportunity to seek the voice of God and find the solace I so desperately needed. What you now hold is the culmination of that precious time *"away with God."*

Writing has always been how I best communicated with God, regardless of the kind of book I was called to write. But in this most recent endeavor, being called to write specifically about the peaceful journey, how to cultivate it and then maintain it, has kept me in a place of quiet gratitude and daily well-being. And that's what I needed more than anything else. I hope this book offers peace and a sense of well-being to you as well when you open it each day for a few quiet minutes "away."

My own journey with God hasn't always been easy. I didn't grow up in a family that had a formal religious or spiritual practice. The occasional Sunday morning at church more or less covered it. And when we gathered with the extended family for a holiday meal, an oftentimes drunk uncle said a meandering grace before we passed the potatoes. I had no idea what I was missing out on, that is, until I came into the rooms of recovery where I was guided to find a connection to a Higher Power.

I wasn't at all sure at that time that developing a relationship with "a God of my understanding" was feasible, let alone desirable. What others seemed so eager and able to do escaped me, and I struggled. My struggle wasn't to stay sober but to stay calm and trusting that I was on the right path and all was well. Others fervently tried to give me *"what they had,"* but to no avail. It wasn't until I lived through a failed attempt at suicide that I began to feel the presence of the God who had always been there. And then we began our connection through the written word, one that wholly sustains me when I turn my attention in His direction each day.

I find it interesting the measures to which God is willing to go to get our attention. I surely don't mean to imply that God initiated the suicide attempt, but He interrupted me in its midst when He sent Pat, a woman I had never seen before, to my door. Her words were the turning point for me. And my life began to include God in a way that had never before been true. However, my "conversations" were often tucked in the middle of the words I happened to be writing. I've never doubted that God chose this path as the right one for me. And thirty-one books later, He has continued to choose it.

It has occurred to me on many occasions that my inability to have children was part and parcel of the work that has been my life. I "have birthed thirty-one children." And each one was as special as the one preceding it. I don't know if it's fair to say that I have been as proud of my books as a mother is of her children, but I do know that each one has felt quite miraculous to me. Indeed, God does work in mysterious ways.

I'm not sure what your approach to reading a daily meditation book is, but there are no wrong ways to do it. Opening the book at random is what some prefer to do. Starting by reading the messages on those special days in one's life, like birthdays, anniversaries, or significant past and future events appeals to some who have written to me over the years. Read it however makes the most sense to you. Reading the same favored, comforting message over and over is also quite appropriate. Help with finding peace however you can is what this book hopes to offer you.

I do believe we are all called to fulfill specific tasks in this life. I am thrilled that mine has been as a writer. From the first book, up to and including this one, I knew I was answering God's call. It's my hope that you will find as much solace in the reading of these daily meditations as I did in the writing of them. We all deserve peace of mind. We all deserve to live free of doubt. We all deserve to know that God is walking every step of our journey with us. And we all deserve to live free of fear every moment of every day. Those are the intentions of this book. May you experience each of them daily.

May love and joy fill your peaceful heart from this day forward.

—Karen
May, 2021

We are always in the right place at the right time.

What a comforting idea this is; it's one I cherish and repeat to myself often. Most of us reading this have perhaps grown accustomed to this idea, but there are days in our lives when we simply need to remember it again. Repeat it often. And share the idea with others so that we keep it uppermost in our minds.

Why is it that we so frequently forget the tiny, profound ideas that can keep us feeling calm and in the "midst of God?" I have come to believe that it's the ego that doesn't want me to remember how close at hand God is. It also doesn't want me to be at peace. Never does it want me to experience peace. I embrace the idea that my mind contains two voices which vie for my attention every moment. One softly says, "All is well and perfect as it is." The other one screams, "*He* is causing this problem you perceive. Go after him."

Fortunately, we have the capacity to choose, over and over again, the voice we prefer hearing.

Let's be careful today. Every moment will be offering us a choice, and that choice makes all the difference in the kind of experiences today will bring.

JANUARY

1.

Detachment is observing people without judgment.

Detaching from the behavior of others might well be one of the most challenging assignments that confronts us on a daily basis. It's not unusual to want to change the behavior of someone else. Sometimes it's a loved one we want to change. It can be a neighbor, a friend, or even a total stranger. The reality is that we simply want to be in control for the sake of what we mistakenly think is our own well-being. Alas, we will never meet with success. We might convince a loved one to do it our way once or twice, but, even then, it's folly to think we now have permanent control.

Detaching from others, letting them be, simply allowing them to behave as they choose, frees us to focus on the only person we can take charge of: our own self. And the relief that letting go allows us to experience makes it easier to let go the next time too. Trying to control anyone else can become habitual. But success will never be lasting. The irony is that failing is actually how we discover what peace feels like.

The quickest avenue to peace is by letting our loved ones live as they choose. Today is a good day to begin.

2.

To avoid pain at all costs forces us to reject half the lessons life can teach.
—Jan Pishok

Life is a series of lessons, and not all of them please us in the moment. But all of them are meant for us. They have been "preapproved" for this lifetime—this journey. Choosing when we learn them is up to us, of course, but they will revisit us until we surrender to them. How lucky we are that we can choose when that moment of surrender will be.

If an experience is painful, might it be due to our resistance to it? Surrendering to the rhythm of an experience (and every experience does have its own rhythm) allows us to flow with the deeper meaning of the inherent lesson. No lesson is ever meant to harm us. But every experience holds a lesson we need in order to become all that we have agreed to be on this journey.

Always remember that no experience, whether painful or loving, is ever superfluous. And never is one of them accidental.

Resist no lesson, whatever the momentary pain might be, and watch your life blossom.

3.

Turning the other cheek doesn't mean giving up our right to respond.

Turning the other cheek is an interesting idea, one I have tried to master throughout my many years in Al-Anon. Unfortunately, I still get sucked into what I interpret as an attack from others on occasion. I have learned, however, that responding in kind or not responding at all are not the only choices. We can respond to any situation from a kinder, more gentle mindset. Remembering what the God of my understanding prefers me to say or do makes a difference in how that situation goes, as well as the rest of my day. This may be true for you too.

Every moment of our lives, we are interacting with others in multiple ways, whether in person, on social media, or even with the folks who drone on and on in newscasts. Allowing ourselves to become negatively engaged doesn't have to be our default response. Turning away can be effective, and, if done respectfully, it can not only change the tenor of the moment for ourselves, but I personally think it can impact millions of others too. Whatever we do or say to one, we actually say or do to all. It's a simple truth, and if understood and integrated into action, one that could rearrange the thinking on the planet.

Choosing how to respond to any instance that presents itself to us today has far-reaching implications. May we all be our better selves.

4.
How important is it?

The tendency to inflate whatever situation isn't developing as I'd planned is a sure way to lose my peace of mind. And I experience this loss on a daily basis, it seems. Even after decades of spiritual work in 12-step rooms and with *A Course in Miracles*, I too easily begin minding the business of someone else, and then my own peace of mind slips away.

The antidote to all of this is to stay focused on the only person and situations I have any control over: those that concern me. It's a very simple equation. Step away from what is not mine to control. Ask myself the question, how important is this really? And in the large scheme of things, nothing is really so important that I can't make the saner choice to move on and let it be. Let others take charge of what is theirs to attend to. And the real gift in this is my own freedom to be at peace.

Every time a circumstance nags at me — or you — it's an opportunity that has come calling, an opportunity to honestly ask, "Is this mine to handle?" I have discovered that on a daily basis, there are really very few things I am called on to handle. The rest are simply situations that belong to others, situations that you and I can quite peacefully observe.

Remembering to ask the tiny question, "How important is it?" can change everything about how this day will unfold. Our lives can be so much simpler. Let's allow them to be.

5.
We grow in darkness and in light.
— Marilyn Mason

Walking through the darkness is familiar to me. Perhaps it is to you too. Even in childhood I felt doomed for periods of time, and, even at eighty-one, I wouldn't say I've gotten used to it. I'm still troubled by the dark periods, but they nevertheless come. What I do know as an adult on this spiritual path is that I will reach the light again. It will come, just as mysteriously as the darkness descended.

I didn't have a safe haven as a child. My feelings of fear and confusion were discounted by the adults in my life, so I never really knew why they came or if they would leave. Consequently, for long stretches, I wallowed in fear. And I wallowed alone.

What has changed? I now believe that God is available to walk with me through the darkness, that in fact, the darkness encourages me to embrace friendship with God, a friendship that will never be denied me. And I know now that the light is just over the hill or around the next corner. It's coming toward me even when I am in the pit of darkness.

My growth as a spiritual being is enhanced by the darkness. And the light then helps me give away the growth that has come. Always there will be growth.

Growth is guaranteed through every experience we have. As a matter of fact, that's the reason for each experience coming our way.

6.

I will always get the experiences I need— whether I want them or not.

The above idea is seldom easy to swallow. In fact, many of us resist this idea repeatedly. And the end result is that we live in perpetual dismay. "But this isn't what I counted on," we think. "What I had in mind was a new job or a different relationship, or possibly more money." Yet living every day becomes so much easier when we make the decision, as we finally must, to embrace the idea that God always has our *better selves* in mind when experiences, which are His gifts to us, arrive in our lives.

Our egos struggle against the idea that God makes better decisions for us. But that has been true throughout our lives. It's helpful to revisit our past and see the many times that God made an appearance by sending us an experience that we were sure was the wrong one, yet our lives took a fortuitous turn. I can count them in the dozens. If I seriously made a list, it would probably be in the hundreds, maybe the thousands. God has always been present. And that fact will never change, never ever—not for any one of us.

I can rest peacefully today knowing that what I need will surface. I also know that God had a hand in it.

7.

Is there ever any particular spot where one can put one's finger and say, "It all began that day, at such a time and place, with such an incident"?
—Agatha Christie

Because our lives are a composite of myriad intersecting events, it's not easy to pinpoint which particular episode in the drama making up our lives was the turning point that made all the difference. And does it finally matter? I think not. We are where we are by design. That's really the fact of our lives that counts.

I certainly didn't embrace this idea before I came into the rooms of recovery. As far as I could see, life was willy-nilly. And that suited me just fine. I didn't know what I was missing. But now living by a different set of principles offers such ease and peace of mind. I have come to cherish the belief that each and every incident was its own turning point. We are where we are right now because of the cumulative impact of all of the incidents, and nary a one of them came to us without the hand of God being involved. Hallelujah.

Wherever our activities take us today, we do not travel solo. How lucky can we be?

8.

Happiness is a byproduct of an effort to make someone else happy.
—Gretta Brooker Palmer

What we give to others, we receive in kind. How simple is that? Our wish to experience happiness will always be honored if we are willing to honor someone else in a manner that makes them happy.

This is not a very complicated equation for living. Yet how often we sit and wait for someone else to make us happy.

Taking to heart how simple the decision to assure ourselves of happiness is what makes our past moments of anguish spent waiting for someone else to shower us with attention or love seem like such a waste of time. *We will receive what we give.* In fact, any act of loving attention which results in happiness for a friend or even a stranger has an immediate payback. Give it a try and see how this works in your life. What we give we do receive!

Today promises to make me happy if I offer the gift of making someone else happy too. This act will never, ever fail us.

9.
God grant me serenity, please.

There is no troubling situation facing us that cannot be alleviated or at least made manageable by seeking serenity and God's help. We simply need to admit that we can't handle most situations alone. It's probably more honest to say that every experience we face is made easier by holding the outstretched hand of God. We were never expected to navigate the twists and turns of our lives solo.

It helps me to remember that God is well aware of every situation I am going through without my even seeking His guidance. And nothing actually comes to us that we haven't been prepared for. The turn of events in our lives has been divinely orchestrated. That's music to my ears; I can give up worry, if I so choose. I can let go of my need to control, if that's my choice. I can simply bask in the knowledge that God is present and will always be as close as my memory of Him.

Our lives can be far easier than many of us choose to live them. The availability of God's help, which assures us of the serenity we seek, is close at hand.

I will take advantage of God's help today and reap the benefit of serenity.

10.

**Continuous effort, not strength or intelligence,
is the key to unlocking our potential.**
—Liane Cordes, *The Reflecting Pond: Meditations for Self-Discovery*

I love this quote. Every one of us can be more than we are at any given moment in time if we put effort into the goals we have set for ourselves. We learn through 12-step programs that it's our job to put in the effort, but God is in charge of the outcomes. However, I think we can influence the outcome by the amount of genuine effort we put forth. The underlying message is loud and clear: we are equal as humans. What we do to unlock our potential is up to each one of us.

Does the quote mean that strength and intelligence are unimportant? I don't think so. But alone, they won't pull us over the finish line. Our effort, our perseverance to keep moving forward, is what's really necessary if we want to become all that we have been created to be.

Today offers us another opportunity to commit to the effort to accomplish the goal we feel called to complete. We won't be alone as we push forward.

11.

**Every loving thought is true; everything else is an appeal
for healing and help, regardless of the form it takes.**
—*A Course in Miracles*

I think this statement is one of the most powerful ideas I have ever encountered. And I'm so grateful that my spiritual journey broadened to include *A Course in Miracles* more than three decades ago. The principles embodied in the course are comfortably complementary to the 12-step programs that have been guiding me for forty-five years. And this particular idea helps me daily to back away from responding too quickly to what I perceive as an attack.

If I choose to interpret every *"unloving"* comment or action as an appeal for help, I can change two lives in that moment: mine and the other person's, by how I respond. How much easier it is to back away or step aside from a perceived "attack" if I can see it as a cry for help. And every response made by anyone, ever, is either a loving one or a cry for help. Always. There is nothing very complicated about this idea.

Today promises to offer hundreds of opportunities to interpret the actions or words of others. My response will make all the difference in the world.

12.
I must be prepared before the crisis comes.
—Ruth Humlecker

Being prepared before something happens may seem counterintuitive. However, those of us who are on a spiritual journey, and I'd venture to say that anyone reading this is, understands the underlying meaning. How do we stay prepared for whatever any day brings? By staying aligned with the God of our understanding. We know without a doubt that with God, all things are possible. We also know that we will never be given more than *both of us together* can handle.

You may remember when you first heard that statement. I couldn't wrap my mind around it. It seemed like I had experienced a lot of things earlier in my life that had overwhelmed me. I hadn't handled them easily. And then I realized that feeling overwhelmed was the result of my not letting God be a part of my journey.

Just hearing that I would never be given more than I could handle didn't ring true. And yet, I survived every dark experience. I gradually was willing to consider that God had intervened and handled everything for me. I didn't have to "*know it*" to make it true.

We are always prepared if we include God in our experiences throughout the day. Nothing can overwhelm Him. Thus, nothing needs to overwhelm us.

No crisis will be too big for God and me to handle today.

13.

**God's messages can reach our ears when we listen attentively
to both friends and strangers. No one we encounter is exempt.**

Rapt attention to others, closing the gap that our egos construct,
is what makes way for the loving messages that God is sending us.
Celebrating our connectedness is the one true pathway to God.
Embracing the awareness that every person we encounter has come
with a message that we need to hear, a message that is specific to
our journey, is the pathway to breathing deeply and securely.

How much easier the journey would be if we simply sat back
and accepted who and what stands before us as the next perfect
opportunity for the growth we have been born to experience.
Remember, *no one* comes unbidden. What is said is what we
need to hear.

Let's be at peace in every encounter today. Each one is perfect as it is.

14.

**Everything in life that we really accept undergoes a change.
So suffering must become love. That is the mystery.
— Katherine Mansfield**

Acceptance of any situation promises us a powerful transformation.
According to the *Big Book of Alcoholics Anonymous*, acceptance is the
answer to all problems. It is the solution for any challenge that
confronts us. Yet surrendering, as we must finally agree to do, is not
always easy. Too often we are seduced into thinking that if we try
just one more time to make a situation fit our expectations, we will
succeed in mastering the problem. We will succeed in making our
lives be what we had counted on them being.

Alas, we are not in control of anything but our own efforts. And
that's the good news! Giving the rest to God allows us to relax
into the solution that's perfect for this and every situation. It is
transformed for the betterment of all, and even more importantly, *we*
are transformed too.

Life really can be so much more peaceful than many of us are currently living it. It's all about acceptance. That decision changes everything in our life — today and every day.

15.

It just doesn't matter.
— Comedian Bill Murray

Recently I saw an interesting Netflix documentary about Bill Murray. Apparently, for some time now, he has been showing up unannounced at parties, weddings, and gatherings of all kinds. He's not there as a celebrity but as just another "guest." The fellow who did the documentary had heard stories about him. After tracking him down, he started following him. What we as viewers get to observe in this documentary is the extraordinary made very ordinary. And Bill's approach to all of it is: It just doesn't matter.

Ever since watching the documentary, I've been intrigued by the idea that nothing really matters in the larger scheme of life. What will be, will be. To embrace the idea that "it just doesn't matter" changes how we respond to any experience that pays a visit. We don't have to overreact. Ever. We don't have to react at all, in fact. Because it just doesn't matter. What a concept for changing lives. What a concept for embracing peace. What an easy choice this actually is.

I choose peace today. I will affirm that "this, too, just doesn't matter."

16.

Forgiveness is the path to peacefulness.

We are allowing ourselves to be held hostage by everyone we are holding a resentment against. We have to explore the ramifications of agreeing to this predicament. What does it even mean to be held hostage on a daily basis? And is it worth it? Is being trapped by the past, and by the behavior of someone not even currently "here," worth the loss of peace and the emotional energy we spend on him or her?

No other experience can get our full attention if we are emotionally preoccupied by the past behavior of someone else. In other words, whatever is happening *now* is slipping through our fingers, never to be experienced again. How sad. How very sad. When the past has us in its grip, when some person from the past continues to take up space in our minds, we have forsaken all possibility of experiencing peace.

We must forgive. We must let go. We must choose to live in the here and now. We must, or we are forsaking any hope of peace today or ever.

17.
Self-control is one of the greatest skills I've learned.
—Jim Burns

What is it about self-control that's so important to our lives? From my aging perspective, it's key because it means I can always make a choice as to how to respond to any experience that grabs my involvement. Nothing "out there" has the power to take over my mind and its reaction. Being in charge of my responses gives me the opportunity to ensure I will be as peaceful as I make up my mind to be.

Choosing peace instead of agitation, which was the place I used to call "home," is so refreshing. Can I make the right choice with every opportunity that comes along? Unfortunately, no. But being able to make the choice to walk away, either literally or in my mind, lessens the angst I sometimes feel.

We simply don't take advantage of our self-control in far too many instances, and the result is a life that's too often troubled as well as generally agitated. There is another way to live, however. And we can hone this tool—beginning now.

I look forward to a peaceful day today. My choices will ensure it.

18.
No experience comes to us unbidden.

Ouch. This isn't always an easy pill to swallow. Most of us can think of all kinds of experiences that we abhorred, in the midst of them. And yet, making the decision to look at how each experience actually fit into the tapestry that made up our lives encourages us to accept this idea. In fact, from my perspective, it's an idea that's worth celebrating.

I think many of us have come to believe in retrospect that what has unfolded as our life has been quite perfect. We have met the learning partners who launched us into the directions we needed to explore in order to become who we are today. I know that not a single experience I had was superfluous to the journey I now celebrate as mine. Even those incidents that were momentarily discouraging, even frightening on occasion, are nestled quite comfortably into the person I am now. I dare to say the same is true for you.

Today, let's take stock of our journey so far. It will allow us to see without a shadow of doubt that our lives have unfolded perfectly.

19.
Every person is your teacher.
—Florence Scovel Shinn

How comforting this thought is to me. It means we are always in the company of people we need to experience—always! I can remember many people throughout my journey who I didn't appreciate at the time when we were interacting. And yet, in hindsight, if I'm honest in my assessment of the encounters, they were advantageous to my learning curve—even those interactions that felt invasive and uncomfortable at the time.

All I have to do is remember this idea when I navigate the hours ahead of me each day. I may not initially feel appreciation for a person who is crossing my path, but she is there to help me fulfill my purpose in this life. Every person is helping us be all that we have been created to be. How divine is the journey. How perfect are our encounters. How necessary are the lessons we are both learning and passing on to others. The absence of any encounter, any teacher, ultimately affects the journey of everyone.

We are connected, one and all. Each person's lessons will in time touch every other person too. What a magnificent plan God has designed.

20.
Simply be an expression of kindness and watch how your day unfolds.

Leading from a place of kindness makes all the difference in how we feel. We can't experience peace if we allow an agitated mind to rule our lives. And the added plus to leading from a place of loving kindness is that love comes back to us. We do receive what we give, if not immediately, at an even better time.

There are so many simple ways to be kind. It begins with making the decision to treat others as you'd like to be treated. Making a call to a friend is an easy action and one that takes only a moment to do. Perhaps praying for someone you have been holding a resentment against is something you may feel able to choose. Ultimately, this will be as loving to you as to him. Another act of kindness that I feel is easy to do is to smile and ask others who are serving me in any place how their day is going. If they are wearing a name tag, calling them by name honors them.

It's not beyond the capabilities of any one of us to be kind to everyone we meet, or live with, or used to be good friends with. Even those we no longer consider friends are worthy of our kindness. We are the better for it.

Having made the decision to show up as an expression of kindness wherever we go today is actually quite easy. All we have to do is try this out once to see how good it feels.

21.

Something needs to be done in the course of a day.
—Edith Shannon

What an interesting yet quite reasonable and simple idea this is. Each day offers an invitation to be involved, and involvement means being engaged in an activity, either with others or alone. Being withdrawn from life can lead to discouragement or even depression for some people. But how quickly a person's attitude changes by doing even one small thing. How quickly doing one small thing fills us with inner peace.

When I used to manage a big company, I often faced a mound of paperwork before the day even got started. And I'd briefly recoil. But I learned that picking up one piece of paper and dealing with one problem or situation at a time, freed me to truly enjoy the rest of the day and all the "invitations" it presented. Doing one task makes every other task seem manageable.

In truth, we are lucky that we do have tasks to handle every day. It means our lives still matter. Let's be grateful that we know that.

Having something that needs to be done by me today makes getting up all the more inviting.

22.

Everything passes, and as I flow with this river of highs and lows, I become calm.
—Ruthie Albert

There is perhaps no greater gift to help us feel the peace we all crave than the reminder that everything passes. I well remember seeing slogans galore when I first entered the rooms of AA and Al-Anon in the mid-seventies. *This Too Shall Pass* was one of the first ones that caught my attention. Initially, I didn't actually grasp its meaning. The idea of simply choosing not to worry and allowing a situation to slip away was beyond my comprehension.

Now I treasure the wisdom of this idea. It does calm my mind. And it's true. Everything does pass. Even the quarantine we are all living with now will pass when the time is right. Giving up the compulsion to fret over everything is such freedom. And as I age, I crave greater periods of quiet peace. I know now that they are mine whenever I want them.

Becoming calm, even in the midst of turmoil, is a choice. All will be well. In time.

23.
We don't see things as they are, we see them as we are.
—Anais Nin

Whether it's conscious or unconscious, we see other people and the constant flow of situations we encounter through our own projections. In other words, we see whatever is "out there" as we want to see it. And this is based solely on how we are feeling in that moment.

Being able to free ourselves of this way of living in the world relies on willingness, first of all. Do we really want to see others as they are? Do we really want to see situations free of our interpretations of what they *should be?*

Living free from our own constant judgment of the world outside of us, which of course colors how we perceive it, takes Herculean effort. It's far easier to let our misperceptions choose for us how to see. But living from this frame of reference prevents us from ever seeing the truth of who people are and what the experiences we have been invited to join really are as well. We can make another choice. And that's the power we each have that's tucked away in our willingness.

Seeing from a fresh perspective today can be our choice. Seeing truth awaits us.

24.
Forgiveness pays many dividends.

We can't overestimate the importance of our willingness to forgive ourselves and those we think have wronged us. In the final analysis, it is the only path to peace of mind. Holding a resentment against another passenger on this journey we share holds us hostage to a time and a place that is long gone. Allowing for the missteps of others frees us to accept our own missteps too.

No one is exempt from making mistakes, and many of our mistakes will infringe in some way on someone else's navigation through life. That's simply the human condition. We are not perfect. We are teachers and students, and it's a fact that some of our mistakes teach us, as well as others, the value of forgiveness. It is the surest way to close the gap that too often exists between us.

Forgiveness forges oneness. It is the glue that holds the human community together. When we resist the opportunity to forgive someone, we are, in the big picture, hurting a multitude of people. What we do or don't do for one affects the entire human community.

The far-reaching impact of every action is referred to as the butterfly effect. The act of forgiveness blesses all life. It's an amazing gift to make a part of your life.

25.
Everything that happens is for my good.

This is a very bold statement. Can it be true? Many would say no. There was a time in my past when I too would have disagreed with it. But the spiritual principles that have been guiding me for more than four decades have changed many of my old beliefs. Now I see from a new perspective. Now I see that there is, and always has been, a divine story unfolding in my life; a story that is perfect in every way. And it's a story that is carrying me to the exact places I need to be, experiencing just what I need to encounter and with the "teachers" I need to learn from. The story will continue until my time is done.

Because of hindsight, we can all see that something in our past that troubled us at the time has now seeded itself into the learning curve, an arc that has been quite perfect for the person we have been and are still becoming. This will continue to be true. Knowing this lessens the hold fear and confusion have on our lives. We are being guided—always. We can trust this.

Whatever draws our attention today is purposeful. It's part of the story unique to each one of us. How comforting that is.

26.
People who think too much about themselves miss many wonderful opportunities to help others.
—Alpha English

We all know people who fall into this category. And we find ourselves there too occasionally. But just knowing our tendency to be self-absorbed can help us take a step back and refocus our attention on others. The people who cross our paths are not there by chance. That's not an easy thing to remember, but it's true. Whether or not we like a particular person who has entered our space is irrelevant. He is there because it's time for us to share an experience.

If we could just remember that we are here as helpmates to others. Even if we only remembered that on occasion, we'd be adding benefit to the world we share with nearly eight billion people.

It's an awesome responsibility we have, isn't it? But it's not beyond the capacity of any one of us to make a commitment upon arising to seek to see the opportunities to help others that present themselves on a daily basis.

Seeing my experiences today with clarity will allow me to help those who show up who need my help. My own spirit will be helped too.

27.
Needing others isn't a failing. It's a gift.

We aren't meant to walk through life in isolation. And needing others to help us live out the journey we are meant to have doesn't mean we are needy. *Neediness* is far different from simply needing the others who are here on our path by design. They come to help us. Without them, we'd be shortchanged in the cycle we were born to complete.

Neediness, on the other hand, means that we are clinging to others, fearful of walking the path that is ours to walk. Neediness blinds us to the actual opportunities for growth that visit us daily. Neediness stunts that growth, which of course means we aren't able to serve as teachers for the others we were born to help.

Other travelers need us as teachers just as we need them. That give-and-take is what ensures that each one of us will become the people God intended us to be. God never fails to orchestrate the encounters needed in each of our lives.

Choosing to be grateful for the gift that every other person is will make our "classroom" today all that it needs to be.

28.
Our words, unless loving, need not be spoken.

This shouldn't even need to be said. However, we no doubt find ourselves saying something nearly every day that we could well have left unsaid. And we hear others doing the same. Oftentimes it's people in positions of influence expressing very unloving thoughts, generally about others they deem of lesser importance. Even though they may not be speaking about us, their words sting. No one is unhurt by the unloving words so often uttered by ourselves and others.

How do we avoid saying words that cut to the quick when heard by others? It's really not that hard, but we have to be willing to pause before saying what first comes to mind and ask ourselves, are these words kind? Am I about to say something that will injure someone else's feelings? Do I need to say what's on the tip of my tongue now? Can I get quiet and choose again, deciding to say something kind or loving instead? If not, can I simply be quiet?

It takes so little to change who we are in the moment. And when we make a choice that's loving and kind, we feel so much better. So does the person we were about to speak to.

I will be very careful with my words today. Unless they are loving, they will not be said.

29.

We can't hear God's voice when we are judging someone.

One of the most beneficial things I have learned from my study of *A Course in Miracles* is that we have two voices in our minds. The one that speaks in a loud, demanding way is the ego's voice. The course says the ego always speaks first and is always wrong. Alas, we still listen to it quite regularly.

The other voice, however, is the voice of the Holy Spirit. And, according to course principles, it was placed in our minds by God, and it conveys to us the direct thoughts of God. It then follows that when we are in the midst of judging someone, we have turned our attention to the ego, which of course it loves. It goes into full gear and commandeers our minds, preventing us from hearing God in that moment.

The good news is that the Holy Spirit holds no grudges. It never judges us for our inattention. It simply waits for us to once again turn our attention back to it. And then we will know the peace that was always ours to experience.

I can decide which voice I want to lead my thoughts and actions today. That's a great opportunity to exercise each and every day.

30.

We're all recovering; we're growing out of the old and into the new.
—Jan Lloyd

Change is the constant in life. And few of us relish it. What we forget is that change is our pathway to growth, sometimes in the workplace, sometimes in family relationships, and generally at a very personal level. We find ourselves resisting change because of our fear that what's on the other side of it will make us unhappy.

Perhaps we feel inadequate about the change before even knowing what it will look like.

If only we could remember that no change comes to us unbidden. Every change that presents itself is part of the divine timeline of our lives, a timeline that we ourselves *formulated* as perfect for our growth.

Whatever change presents itself is what must come if we are to grow into who we were born to be. Change is a reason for celebration.

Today I will remember that I face nothing alone. And I will remember that every experience has been honed perfectly for my growth and with my input.

31.

All problems can be handled by changing our minds about them.

We so often stay focused on what we think our problems are that we exaggerate them, making it far more difficult to discern their solution. What we tend to forget is that within every problem *is* the solution. More specifically, all it finally takes to solve any problem is our willingness to change our mind about how we see the situation we are defining as a problem.

Whatever we confront in life is always a learning opportunity. To decide to interpret every situation from that perspective eliminates the feeling that it's even a problem at all. Our minds have such power, and utilizing them in a positive way changes every instant of our lives. Being reminded that we can change our minds and, that if we do, our lives will change as well may perhaps seem too simple. But it's true.

To decide, for this day only, to see only opportunities unfolding before us would heal us in untold ways. Being stuck in our old way of thinking—defining everything as a problem—makes life very difficult. To choose to see differently, just for today, would be mind-altering—and oh so good for the soul.

By the way I choose to see the myriad situations in my life today, I can live far more peacefully. Every moment is just another opportunity for joy.

FEBRUARY

1.

**To show great love for God and our neighbor,
we need not do great things.
—Mother Teresa**

I love the simplicity of this idea. Simply being kind and helpful to
the next person we encounter is showing great love for God. I also
remember hearing many years ago that Mother Teresa said, "Love
everyone. And start with the person standing next to you." Our
ability to do both of these things is unquestioned. But do we have
the willingness?

Having the willingness to make a difference in even a small way
could have a very powerful and far-reaching impact. Also, Mother
Teresa's challenge to love everyone is so simple that every single one
of us can do it if only we are willing.

I like believing that it's not the size of our contribution to the others
we encounter that matters. Just showing up, saying "count me in,"
and doing the next right thing is what will shift the way we see one
another. And as one of us changes, others begin to follow suit. Good
deeds don't go unnoticed; they multiply.

*Being willing to take a simple action to make this a better day for someone we
encounter is a challenge that will benefit the giver along with the receiver.*

2.

**Every experience has its perfect place on our life's timeline,
and each one of them is accompanied by God. Let's not fret.**

So many experiences don't quite fit into our plans, do they? But
how fortunate some of us are that we have learned to embrace the
idea that God always has the perfect plan for us to experience,
whether it's one we'd have selected or not.

My past is replete with situations I would rather have avoided at
the time; the ending of my first marriage, for instance. However,

if that event had not occurred, I would not have veered off into multiple very ill-conceived relationships that one by one eventually led me closer to the rooms of Alcoholics Anonymous. The events in my past were perfectly orchestrated and not by me.

We can always count on that to be true. And I know I am exactly where I am supposed to be, right now. How good that feels! I will always be exactly where I need to be. The orchestration of our lives is in good hands.

We may not love what's happening today, but give your resistance a rest. All is in perfect order.

3.

It is important that we plan for the future, imperative that we accept an outcome unplanned.
—Molly McDonald

Planning for the future has its place in our lives. When we want to live responsibly, we need to have some idea about where we want to go. Goal setting is the framework for a life well lived. However, plans go awry. Outcomes don't always match what we expect. And that's when acceptance becomes a crucial response.

I believe that acceptance of however the events we had planned actually unfold is the key to peace of mind. We don't have to like all that we ultimately need to accept, but if we can let go of our resistance to what has presented itself, even for a moment, we will feel relief.

Letting go of our disappointment over an unplanned outcome is always the wise choice. It's also the way to continued growth. And that's what our original plans were all about anyway.

Never forget that God has a part to play in how every event unfolds in our lives. No outcome is actually "unplanned" when we factor God in.

4.

Accepting powerlessness lightens our burdens.

The idea that we can control others is appealing to the uninformed. I spent years thinking that if only I found the right words, I could get another person to change his or her behavior. It led to frustration. Even worse, it led to thousands of futile arguments. I wasn't easily convinced that I couldn't eventually get someone else to see a situation my way.

Alas, it wasn't until I found the rooms of Al-Anon that I got the message that controlling others was an impossibility. And even after finding Al-Anon, I didn't give up trying right away.

Now I can say that embracing powerlessness over all people and sundry situations relieves me of a huge burden. We can't control anyone else, so why not enjoy the fruits of our powerlessness? It gives us more time to simply enjoy every moment of the day. It enhances our relationships with all the people we tried to control. And it means that we can finally experience peace, and after all, isn't that what we were hoping for all along?

Letting others live as they choose is where peace resides. We can have as much peace as we yearn for today. The choice is ours.

5.

Every person is responsible for all the good within the scope of her abilities, and no more.
— Gail Hamilton

Having a daily assignment of simply *doing good* makes life so much more manageable — and pleasant, I might add. There's not a lot to figure out. We merely need to pause before taking any action or saying anything and ask ourselves, "Is this a good response to make at this time?"

Maybe this feels like a complicated way to live one's life, but that's only because most of us are used to shooting from the hip. Being more circumspect about our interactions assures us that we won't be unnecessarily hurting others. Nor will we be getting involved in situations that are not wearing our names.

I believe that doing good simply means being helpful, but not overstepping our bounds. It means bringing a benefit to every situation rather than creating a problem. There is nothing difficult about this suggestion. It's a choice.

Today will present us with many opportunities to offer a helping hand. Are we willing to meet the challenge?

6.
I don't know what the future holds, but I know who holds the future.

A good friend shared this idea with me a few days ago. She had heard it at a 12-step meeting, and I loved it. This concept answers every concern we have. It can take away all of our worries if we embrace it. And I emphatically believe that our future is already divinely laid out. We just don't know the details yet. They will be perfect, however, and exactly what we need for the journey we have already agreed to make.

There really isn't any guesswork in the life we are here to lead. That's not so easy to believe when something dire has just happened. It's so common for us to fall into fear rather than *"falling into God."* But He is always present to alleviate our fears, whatever they are. The future is indeed planned perfectly for us. And He is our guide to walk us through it. What a wonderful feeling this can be if we choose to cherish it.

The future isn't really unknown, except to us. And we need not worry. We have a constant companion to accompany us.

7.
Wherever we go, there we are.
—Earnie Larson

I was at one of his workshops when I first heard Earnie use this phrase. I was flummoxed at the time; I couldn't quite wrap my mind around it. And then it hit me. Of course, we are always carrying *our self* along, the self we have decided to be in whatever moment we are experiencing. If we are angry, guess who accompanies us? If we are full of judgment, guess who is casting that judgment wherever she or he looks? If we are filled with fear, of course we will look out into the world around us fearfully.

It really isn't a mysterious idea. We can only present to the world the composite of how we feel in each moment. The good news, of course, is that we have the capacity to change whoever we are taking wherever we go. And only we can do that. Others can't change us. Maybe the action of someone else will please us, but we will still show up in each moment exactly as we choose to.

Knowing that we have the capacity to be who we want to be wherever we go is a powerful but daunting realization. We are always the decision makers. Take care!

8.
Arrive already loved.
—Mariah Fenton Gladis

A good friend recently shared Mariah's idea at a gathering of friends, and it pleased me in such a profound way. Many of us struggle to believe that we are lovable. Growing up in homes where love felt conditional crippled us for years. And the shadow of how that felt still haunts us occasionally, which means we doubt our acceptance by others in many of the places we visit, even in those places we frequent a lot.

Affirming that we *are already loved* is a mind-bending decision. And it's so refreshing. We are after all in charge of how we see ourselves. We are in charge of what we think of ourselves. And we are in charge of who we are in every situation we gravitate to. To arrive anywhere believing we are already loved makes the experience, no matter what it is, entirely different. We are at peace when we choose to live by this idea as a constant affirmation.

We are loved wherever we go. We can relax. God is our "lover."

9.

Inside me is a stirring truth that is guided by my Higher Power.
— Laurel Lewis

How comforting it is to know that truth lies within us, because
that's where our Higher Power is found, too. In fact, they are one
and the same. We are never estranged from either the truth or God.
However, we can think we have been abandoned by God, which
means we can also believe we have lost our connection to the truth.
That's the direct result of the power of the ego, which doesn't want
us to realize that we are always in the comforting presence of God.

Ego really wants to rule our lives. And many reading this have no
doubt struggled in the past with the ego's attempts to be in charge.
For me, those years were fraught with danger, unhappiness, failure,
and overwhelming fear. Alas, they were all brought on by my
attachment to the ego part of my mind. There was always the other
part, the part that was directly aligned to my Higher Power, but I
too willingly ignored that aspect.

How glad I am that I finally see the light. How glad I am that I can
now choose to hear the truth on a regular basis.

We always have the choice to hear the Truth. Free will is our birthright.
Using it wisely is up to us. Today will offer many opportunities.

10.

When I'm acting as if I'm the center of the universe, it's
helpful to be reminded that I'm just another bozo on the bus.
— Rose Casey

Oh, how we want to be special. Most of us long to be the center of
someone else's life, if not the center of the whole universe. I know
this was my malady for years, and I could find no peace of mind.
My focus was always on the other person in the hope of discovering
that their focus was on me. So many years were wasted watching
others rather than seeking to find God within myself.

But that part of my life is past — I am so grateful. However,
transforming that dynamic took absolute commitment to embracing

the spiritual principle that my Higher Power is always within and always just as available to me as my willingness to go within and converse with Him. What a gift conversing with Him is. I will never fail to know what to do or say now that I've discovered His presence. What a blessing this discovery is.

Today will be as peaceful as my willingness to allow God to decide my words and actions for me.

11.
My satisfaction with myself and my satisfaction with other people are directly proportional.
—Sue Atchley Ebaugh

How we are feeling about someone else, perhaps a friend or a total stranger, a politician or a television personality, or a family member or a neighbor, indicates how we are feeling about ourselves at that moment. We project onto others those feelings we don't want to claim ownership of in ourselves. Truth be told, we have probably been doing this our whole lives. But there is a solution.

We can begin every morning being grateful for even the smallest of things. I remember my mother saying, that when she was the age I am now, she was grateful that she woke up. That always brought a smile to my eyes. To have a friend we can call just to say hello is such a gift. Being grateful that we have a toothbrush to clean our teeth is even worthy of notice. Small things are in reality big things, if we give them the notice they deserve. And the more we count our blessings, the more satisfaction we will feel toward everyone — even ourselves.

I can change my level of satisfaction today in an instant. It begins with embracing gratitude for any one person or thing we have in our lives.

12.
One choice is all we ever need to make.

Can that statement actually be true? One choice? And the resounding answer is *yes*. One choice: and it's the choice to listen to the part of our mind that is linked directly to God. We have always had access to that part, but far too often we allow the "other part" of our mind to sway our thoughts and actions.

In other meditations, I have mentioned that "other part." It's the ego, and it's demanding, not kind nor soft in any way. But we can choose to ignore it. Ignoring the ego takes willingness, however. It doesn't make it easy to shut out its voice, but perseverance is what develops a new habit. Listening to the ego rather than the voice of God was simply a bad habit. Now it's time to commit to a new habit; one that will change our lives completely.

As the saying goes, today is the first day of the rest of our lives. Let's begin by making the kinder choice for ourselves and all the other people we encounter throughout the day.

13.
To not have control over the events that shape our lives is difficult.
—Mary Larson

How we wish we were in control of everything, particularly the people in our lives. But how fortunate we are that that's not the case. Were we in absolute control of all the people and situations we encounter daily, we'd be constantly exhausted. We'd never know peace, not even for a moment.

We may mistakenly think that if we were in charge, we'd always be peaceful; but the reverse is all too true. Although it may be true that having others behave willy-nilly causes us momentary consternation, if we were pulling the strings as though they were our puppets, our work would be unending. Turning everything over to a Higher Power offers such relief. And it's in that act that we discover our lives are not really difficult at all.

Who would have guessed?

Being freed from the need to take charge of others is a gift beyond measure. It's a lifetime of peace.

14.
What is not love is always fear.

This idea seemed too definitive, too uncompromising, when I was first introduced to it in *A Course in Miracles* many years ago. And actually, I also thought it was a much too simplistic way to judge the actions of others. And now, I have grown to love the simplicity of the idea. I can intuit, pretty quickly, when a person is feeling love or fear, and this knowledge helps me make a proper response.

The course has helped me discern what is being reflected by others' actions and words. It has also helped me realize that I have one proper response in all instances: my response should always reflect love. In other words, meet love with love. But even more importantly, meet fear with love too. And when we live with that simple equation as our guide, peace will be available with each breath we take.

At any age, peace seems to be the most desired state of mind. There is one way to assure ourselves of it. Always lead from a place of love.

15.
Give to the world the best you have, and the best will come back to you.
—Madeline Bridge

How simple this suggestion is. But note that it *begins with us*. We take the initiative first in order to give our best. We don't wait for the other person to reach out with kindness before we act kindly. Perhaps this isn't what we have been accustomed to doing, but it's generally true that if we act kindly, we will elicit good responses from others.

Let it begin with me is such a great, very short reminder for bringing good into the many exchanges with others that we have on a daily basis. Whether it's in our family or at the grocery, letting kindness begin with us means that we will never be at a loss about what to do or say. And it puts us in control of a situation in the right way.

We still can't control how others might respond. But we can be pretty certain that if we begin the exchange with kindness, it's more likely we will be met with kindness in return.

We have as many opportunities today as we have encounters with others to make a positive difference in the way life is unfolding for many of us. I will do my part.

16.

We need to give back, to plow something back into the ground.
— Jim Burns

Tilling the soil of humankind is a wonderful image, I think. It's a gentle offering to all members of our human community. It's soothing the moments of discontent with the soft touch of a hoe or a hand. The good among us won't simply be takers. We will choose to be givers too, whenever the opportunity arises.

It takes so very little to make a difference in this universe we share. Not one of us has to be part of a large undertaking. It's the cumulative effect of all of us doing a tiny bit of giving back that adds up to a changed world for everyone. And the need is there. Nothing changes if we don't do anything in a different way. Making the decision to be part of the change for the good is all we need to consider on a daily basis. Just that. Nothing more.

Today will present each one of us with an opportunity to give back. Let's be part of a worthy movement. It only takes a "yes" from us.

17.

To truly love is to free the other person
to be whoever he needs to be.

Loving one another is a gift each of us can offer, not just to our families and friends, but even to the strangers who have yet to become our friends. But when we make the ties of love too tight, preventing the necessary growth each one of us was born to experience, it is no longer actual love; it's imprisonment. And holding someone hostage — or being held hostage ourselves — is the opposite of love. And it's not uncommon, unfortunately.

We can't change how others choose to define love, but we can practice the kind of love that frees others to be fully themselves. Practicing this kind of love ensures us that we are imparting the same kind of love that God offers to each one of us every moment. Loving as God wants us to love is what's being suggested. This is not a complicated request.

Today stands before me awaiting my first move. With God's influence in my life, I can choose to be a giver of love.

18.
We will never hear anyone else's thoughts
if we are only listening to our own.
— Cathy Stone

It's all too easy to fail to recognize that those who are crossing our paths are there as our teachers, quite by design in fact, which means they have very specific guidance they have been *sent* to offer us. However, we have to be willing to listen. It's so very easy to just focus on our own narrow thoughts, ignoring these teachers we had agreed to learn from.

Coming to believe as I have that we serve as one another's teachers makes the multiple *surprising* encounters we experience on a daily basis so much easier to understand. There are no *unintentional* encounters. All exchanges are serving their specific purpose in our lives. But we need to be open to these experiences. Nary a one of them will be repeated in the same way ever again.

Listen up. That's all we have to do today to hear the specifics of what we are here to handle.

19.
Keep it simple.

This little three-word suggestion is a slogan that I was first introduced to in the rooms of Alcoholics Anonymous, forty-five years ago. At the time, I dismissed it as far too simplistic for the likes of me. In all honesty, I didn't even grasp its meaning. I smile every time I think of those days now and of how arrogant I was. I was a PhD candidate then, after all, and I couldn't be helped by something so insipid. Not me!

And today, all these many years later, I hunger for the simpler suggestions for how to live. Keeping life simple, doing just one thing at a time, and listening to just one voice at a time is what allows me to live with grace and many moments of peace. Keeping life simple for this one day only is doable. It means not taking on those activities that are not divinely assigned to me. Let others do what is theirs to do.

Living this way allows us to live with purpose that is ours, and no one else's.

How lucky are we to be given the suggestion to live the simple life. Nothing will overwhelm us today if we stay focused on the simple path.

20.

Filling the hole in our soul with contemplation, meditation, and prayer will teach us that the God of our understanding is there.
—Jan Lloyd

Coming to the belief that God is within me at all times has completely changed my outlook on life. I used to live in dread of the unknown—and it seemed that everything was unknown. But now I celebrate the knowledge that everything is known already and that I will be apprised of what I need to know at the perfect time. What a life-changer this has been for me.

As a child, I lived in constant fear, and the fear didn't subside much until I was in a 12-step program. I think we get imprinted with fear as youngsters if we grow up in a fearful environment. But we can come to know, *and live*, another way. I am proof of that.

Coming to believe that there is a Presence and a Power that truly wants to guide me and protect me has changed everything about my life. Thus, the people I have known over the years have also been impacted by my change of perspective. How much sweeter life is with this knowledge to support me.

God has been within us forever. Let's live in a way that reveals our gratitude for His presence. Let's start now.

21.
Listening is a gift to ourselves.

God is always present to guide me. What an amazing difference this knowledge has made in my life since I came to believe it. Of course, I have to be willing to listen to the words He shares, sometimes through others, sometimes in a passage I am inspired to read. The bumps in the road that occasionally trip me up are due to my resistance to paying attention. God doesn't leave, or change, or go quiet. My willingness to listen is what changes.

Really, it's all so simple. God is here, now. All I have to do is listen. I will never be misled on this journey, but I must follow the guidance that's being offered. There's really nothing complicated about this. God will never quit doing His part. We can do ours just as adamantly—one day at a time.

Today stands before us. Are we willing to listen today? God is waiting.

22.
Lasting friends are precious to me. We seem to help center each other as we travel parallel paths.
—Robyn Halsema

You can't put a price tag on true friendship. And we are not on parallel paths by accident. We are the teachers and the students each of us needs for the growth we have committed ourselves to experiencing on this journey through life.

Looking at our experiences this way makes them all the more meaningful. What I need to know, you help provide. And I do the same for you. We find our way to our proper destination in each other's company.

Perhaps you've never considered just how perfect your circle of friends is. No one has joined the circle accidentally. And each lesson you need to become who you are destined to be has been brought to you by someone in the circle already, or perhaps someone who will soon join it. How exciting to think of our friends and all of our "lessons" in this way. We have need of one another. And this will continue to be true until our journey comes to an end.

What a joy to see all of my friends for who they really are. I will show my appreciation today.

23.

**Wisdom lets us know that the key is not
to judge, but to love and nurture.**
— Jane Nelson

The inclination to judge those who don't think the way we do is so compelling, but eventually so debilitating. Perhaps we grew up in a family where negatively judging others was so common that we didn't even notice it. In fact, it may have been the norm at home. Unfortunately, we do become great imitators of the poor habits of others. But it doesn't have to be this way. We can realize how detrimental our habits are and change them.

Making the choice to nurture others and to express love feels as good to us as it does to those we shower with this kind of attention. We may not grasp this at first, but the more we practice being kind and loving, the more our lives reflect the love. What we give to others does rub off. And others repay us in kind too.

I will be vigilant regarding my actions today. They will impact me as much as others.

24.

**It is imperative that we take a close look at the effect
our thoughts and beliefs have on our lives.**
— Susan Smith Jones

It's possible to live quite unconsciously regarding the impact our beliefs are having on our lives. Everything we do and say is a constant reflection of the thoughts we are protecting. It's quite possible that we aren't even aware that our thoughts are eliciting the experiences we are attracting into our daily lives. But the evidence is there for others to see. Hopefully, we too will see the evidence in time.

Whatever we are thinking creates the world we are seeing, which in turn invites our reaction, and that reaction quite frequently lands us in hot water. Our minds are the culprits. But we aren't prisoners of our minds without our consent. If we want to live a different experience, all we have to do is take charge of our thoughts. A peaceful life requires thoughts that are peaceful. A loving life requires that we nurture loving thoughts and then express them. The formula is a simple one.

Today is a clean slate. My thoughts will determine how graced my day will feel.

25.
Conscience is the perfect interpreter of life.
— Karl Barth

There isn't an action or a thought that we harbor that doesn't speak volumes about who we are in the present moment. But do we want others to know us as we *really* are at our less conscious times? If we hope no one noticed what we just said or did, we no doubt owe an amend. And as long as we are willing to right our wrongs, all can be forgiven. But if we pretend we didn't say or do something ugly, we need to take stock of who we have become and make some changes — immediately.

The fortunate thing about the conscience is that it can't be fooled. Nothing goes unnoticed. But there is nothing about us that can't be changed. That's the good news. We are always in a state of becoming. Let's make sure we are always becoming what God wants us to be. There is no doubt that we know who that is. All that's lacking is the decision to become that person.

Today will be my test run. Will I show up the right way or will I have some amends to make before the day ends?

26.

Let us be willing to release old hurts.
—Martha Smock

The hunger to hang on to past hurts can be extremely seductive. But of course, when we do, we end up stumbling through the moments we are living with blinders on. We actually can't be any place but in the here and now if we want to truly live. That sounds so simple, but it takes a Herculean effort to stay in the moment. Assuredly, that effort relies on having made a serious decision to do so, one to which we may have to recommit many times.

The past can be haunting, for sure, particularly if we were the victim of someone else's ugly behavior. However, keeping that experience alive by reliving it over and over punishes no one but ourselves. Letting go of the past, every moment of the past, regardless of what those moments might have wrought, is the only way to discover the life God is offering us now. We can trust that the offering He is making right now is what will transport us to the next perfect experience we need, one that may right all past wrongs.

Whatever happened in any yesterday of our lives is gone now. Let its memory go and live now.

27.

It is what we all do with our hearts that
affects others most deeply.
—Gerald Jampolsky

What is your heart doing right now? Is it expressing love to all the people who are crossing your mind? Or crossing your path? Is your heart open and reveling in gratitude for all the experiences you have already had, experiences that led you to this moment in time?

Our hearts can be put in charge of our thoughts. Even more importantly, they can be put in charge of our actions. And when we have taken that ever so important step to give our hearts control over who we are or want to become, life changes. And not just our own lives; the lives of those we encounter throughout the day are changed by what our hearts dictate as well.

We can't overestimate how important the involvement of our heart is in every word we speak and every action we take. We will make a valuable difference in so many lives today if we open our hearts and let them lead us into every moment we experience.

What a glorious and peace-filled day we will have if we let our hearts lead the way.

28.
Listening is a wonderful gift with which
we can choose to open each day.

I have heard it said that offering rapt attention to whomever is speaking to us is the gift they deserve. And it's the gift we are deserving of in that very moment too. Listening to whomever comes calling is the very reason someone is crossing our path. Dismissing anyone as unimportant to the journey we are making is folly indeed.

I've said before and it bears repeating, there are no accidental visitors on our path. And this means listen up! There is a message you need to hear, and it's an important factor in where your steps will take you next.

It's really quite exciting when we look at our lives from this perspective. It takes away the guesswork about who is important to our journey and who isn't. If someone has crossed your path, he or she is a very necessary fellow traveler. Don't turn away. Pay attention.

Living with this clarity regarding all who cross our paths makes our life so much easier. No one is without purpose on our journey. No one.

MARCH

1.
Problems are opportunities in disguise.

The ability to change our perception at will is what makes the difference in how one's day develops. If the ego is the one in charge of our perception, we will likely see a host of problems. But we can make a different choice every time a "problem" presents itself. It's really a mindset that is holding us hostage. And we don't have to live in that stranglehold a minute longer—but we have to break free.

The decision to see everything as an opportunity for the growth for which we are now ready is so refreshing. And this is the truth we can live by. We are progressing along a trajectory that is divinely our own, no one else's. We will encounter nothing but opportunities at every step of the journey. Perhaps we have habitually seen situations as problems, but that need not be how we see from this moment on. Nothing is a problem unless we choose to make it one. Nothing.

Today is as problem-free as my willingness to see only opportunities allows. It's my choice, moment by moment.

2.
An ounce of action is worth a ton of theory.
—Friedrich Engels

When a situation presents itself that needs a response, taking action is important, but not just any action. Making a thoughtful response, one that's fitting to the situation, requires that we listen to the inner voice that wants to help us make the right response. Guessing what to do counts for little. However, listening to the softer guidance within will help formulate exactly the right action to fit the situation.

Our lives are an accumulation of a vast number of situations and responses. And every one of them presents itself at exactly the right time for the growth we are ready for. Our lives are unfolding in such an amazing way. Everything comes at the perfect time. And we are always made ready for anything that comes.

No action is necessary unless the inner voice has spoken. It's our job to first be attentive—and then willing.

What comes our way today is perfect. We need not fret about how to handle any of it. If we get quiet, we will know.

3.

Love is a great beautifier.
—Louisa May Alcott

There are a lot of situations in this life we share with family members and friends as well as a host of strangers, situations that need beauty brought to them. Far too often, we carry our cynical selves, our angry selves, or our bullying selves into our encounters with the "teachers" who show up on our path. It's terribly important that we remember that every person who is heading our way, both those we know and those unknown, is *on assignment*.

Frankly, I am relieved that my spiritual guidance has encouraged me to see my life unfolding in this way. I don't ever have to be leery of any special person who has something significant to share with me. *Everyone is paying me a visit because there is a need for their path to cross mine for the lessons we are both ready to learn.* Accepting those lessons with a loving heart is the recipe for making this world we share with so many others a better place. And every time we encourage love to flow from us, we too are changed for the better.

Being a loving presence depends solely on our making the decision to offer the hand of love in every situation that invites us in. We will have multiple opportunities today.

4.

Often God shuts a door in our face and then subsequently opens the door through which we need to go.
—Catherine Marshall

When a door closes as we travel life's path, it's common to feel frustrated. At times, we may even feel fearful because of our confusion. We were certain we were headed in the right direction, and so often the door closes with no forewarning. What's so necessary to remember is that God always has the big picture of our lives on His "screen," and where we need to head next will always be shown to us.

Personally, I am so glad that I have chosen to let God be the director of the orchestra I'm playing in now. I was on the wrong path for a long time with no one but my ego in charge. It was a scary trip that included many detours, each one a bit more uncertain than the previous one. That I came to believe that there was another way to traverse life still amazes me. However, that's the power of God. He closed one final door, and the next one led me to safety.

God will always lead us to safety. We have to choose to follow, however.

We are always being given the guidance that's perfect for us. Let's not veer off course today.

5.

In turbulent times, it's even harder to live a balanced life.
—Sue Ebaugh

Because of the pandemic currently sweeping the world, these times have felt uncertain in many respects. We wonder how safe we are when we leave our homes. We wonder if the next phone call might be from a friend who has tested positive. We wonder if we have all the information we need to live free from disease.

But there is a way to stay sane during this upheaval. And it's to make sure we are keeping the pathway to God's presence uncluttered. Clearing our minds so we can hear His guidance, so we can know the peace that is being offered to us, is the first priority.

Living a balanced life might not look the same for all of us. But taking time for a visit with the God of our understanding must be paramount in every day's activities. That visit, however we approach it, will calm our minds and hearts. Reminding ourselves that God is always present, even in the midst of what's troubling us, is the way out of the chaos that all too easily ensnares our minds.

Turning to God is the solution for everything that disrupts my peace of mind today.

6.

God does not comfort us to make us comfortable but to make us comforters.
—J. H. Jowett

This idea is so gentle, so appealing and so quiet. God is teaching us to do that which He does. How amazing. As we feel comforted, we have the inner peace to be a comforting presence in the lives of others. That's why the others have headed our way, in fact. They have been attracted to our comforting demeanor because of their need to be at peace. In our own peace, we can offer peace to others.

Because we have welcomed God into our lives, we can give to others all that God has given to us. And the priceless gift we have received and will keep receiving, as long as we keep our hearts open, is peace. There need never be chaos in our lives again. As long as we keep God in our minds, we will know peace.

Having the opportunity to offer others what God has offered us is the very reason we are alive. What a holy experience we have been promised.

I will be in the circle of the sacred today. God will show me how to comfort all who wander my way.

7.

I long to accomplish a great and noble task, but it is my chief duty to accomplish small tasks as if they were great and noble.
—Helen Keller

Helen Keller is quite possibly the epitome of humility. She was an amazing woman who didn't let her disabilities, which were acute, interfere with her achieving great things. She took things as they were, not as she might have preferred them to be, and moved forward with acceptance. We could all profit from learning that lesson.

Whatever the circumstances of our life, they are what has been orchestrated for us in this moment of time. Making the decision to believe this changes everything about how we navigate the rough waters we might encounter. There will be rough waters ahead, that's the nature of life. But we will never be expected to navigate them alone. And any task that is ours to accomplish has been explicitly sent to us because we can handle it. God is and always will be available to walk us through or carry us over the troubled waters.

No task, large or small, needs to feel daunting. If it is presented to us, we can certainly handle it.

8.
Now, this very moment, is all there is.

What a simple statement. Yet what an elusive concept it communicates, one almost beyond my capacity to fathom. I'm not a newcomer on this spiritual path, in fact, my journey in 12-step recovery began in 1974. That is quite an accumulation of "moments" I have experienced; they number in the millions, perhaps the tens of millions. And yet I'm embarrassed to admit that I have missed most of them. Why is that? Because I was trapped in a past experience or already contemplating a future one.

When I do connect with "now," I feel a ripple passing through my body. I remember when I read *The Power of Now* by Eckhart Tolle I felt connected to a Higher Source in a new way, a connection I was certain I'd never lose. Alas, it slips through my fingers on a daily basis. But *the moment* can be reclaimed by making the decision to just pause and rest in this particular moment. I can make the decision to clear my mind of the thoughts that clutter my senses. Simply let them go. Let everything go. And feel the freedom to live in joy.

I can be at peace in the moment. All I have to do is claim it.

9.

Doing what is right isn't the problem; it's knowing what is right.
—Lyndon B. Johnson

We really do know what's right. After eighty-one years, I'm pretty convinced of this. But if we feel momentarily unsure, all we have to do is pause and allow the inner voice which always helps us lead from the heart to take charge. Being the loving presence in every situation is the right choice, and it's what helps the other people who are present to feel at ease.

There is no mystery when it comes to knowing what's the right thing to do. We feel it instantly, and we can act on that feeling with the assurance that our actions are in accord with what God wants us to be. However, it's always a matter of choice. Are we going to let the ego decide our actions, or are we going to seek another director for the drama playing out in our lives?

There is nothing complicated about knowing what's right. It has been clear to us since the first time we made any decision at all. Our problem is walking away from the right choice.

We can make only right choices today. It's really quite simple.

10.

There are two kinds of business:
my business and none of my business.
—Richie E.

I heard this amazingly simple idea at an Al-Anon meeting a number of years ago. And I took it as gospel. Unfortunately, I still often cross the line between the business that is mine and that which clearly belongs to someone else. But I can see the error of my ways more quickly now. And that's progress.

Of course, the reason this is such an important idea is that it allows those people who wander onto our path to be in charge of their own lives. When we mistakenly think that their closeness is an invitation for us to get involved in their decisions, we create tension—or worse.

It's far too easy to drive others away when we try to make their business our own. Even more importantly, when we mind someone else's business, we take on a burden that complicates our own journey. Walking away is the best decision when we feel ourselves getting pulled in.

Just for today, stay out of the way of someone else's business. It's really not that hard. It just takes willingness.

11.
It takes time, love, and support to find peace.
—Deidra Sarault

The search for peace is undoubtedly the most important leg of any one's journey. And it will be found. Peace has been promised to us. However, we have to be willing to give up anger and control to find it. Our decision to detach from the chaos and static that we often encounter when others cross our path is the key to finding the peace that we so deserve.

If only the decision to give up our anger and control were easily accomplished, there would be no more skirmishes in families, in neighborhoods, or between countries. But it takes willingness to see situations that engender unrest within us in a different way. It has been suggested that all we have to do is make the request: *Help me see this a different way.* And then wait for the shift in our vision and our mood to occur. It will. Absolutely.

Today can be gently peaceful, from morning until we lay our heads down to sleep. It's up to us.

12.
Do nothing without the counsel of God.

This suggestion doesn't offer a lot of wiggle room. We either seek God's guidance or we don't, and the outcome of the situation will either be smooth or it won't. I don't mean to imply that every outcome will please us in the moment, even when it's orchestrated by God, but we will see that it was the right outcome as time passes.

Never will we be led astray by God. And we are often led astray when we listen to the guidance of the ego. The unfortunate reality is that the ego is accustomed to us listening to it, and its messages are relentless.

We have to want to hear the softer voice of God. But it's our choice. The obvious questions to ask ourselves are: Do I want to know peace? Do I want to serve as a peaceful presence in the lives of others? If the answer is yes, listen only to God. And all will be well.

There is nothing complicated about how to approach this day that stands before us. Be present to God and it will unfold perfectly.

13.
Seek to see the peaceful side of everyone.

This may seem like a tall order when we consider some of the people who frequently cross our paths. And yet, everyone does have a peaceful side. We will see it if we choose to look. It is said that who we see is ourselves. That idea may make us uncomfortable if we take it to heart. And we should take it to heart. How we are feeling, moment by moment, is who we are actually projecting, thus it's who we see.

We can always test this to see how accurate this idea is. Evaluate your own mood right now, then see how your mood influences how you see the next person who crosses your path. And if you need an attitude adjustment, make one and then retest yourself. It's pretty accurate that who you see is a reflection of how you choose to see the world and all its inhabitants. The more content you are, the more peaceful all your encounters will become.

Our perceptions of others tell us who we are. Is it time for an attitude adjustment?

14.
Help me see this differently.

The quickest way to a peaceful mind is to willingly ask God for help to see whatever stressful situation has claimed our attention differently. I can assure you that your entire mood will change from agitated to peaceful when you allow God to change your mind. And in the final analysis, our primary purpose in this life is to be helpful to one another—period. And doing it from a place of love is the kindest way to show up in the life of anyone else.

Seeking to see a situation differently is such a simple request of God. We can be completely certain that our request will be heard and answered. God wants us to be peaceful, and He wants us to be helpful too. We simply have to be willing to seek the help. How easy is that?

If I need an attitude adjustment today, there is a solution. God is always waiting to help. But I must ask.

15.
An appeal for healing and help is not always obvious.
We often mistake it for anger, an outright attack, or bullying.

This idea is one of the most helpful ideas I was ever introduced to, and it was my study of *A Course in Miracles* which really enlightened me about the meaning behind the behavior of others. I certainly recognized people's anger; I was the daughter of an angry man. And being attacked is an unmistakable experience, whether verbally or physically. However, allowing myself to see these outbursts as an appeal for help has changed me in a profound way.

I no longer think others really want to be angry or abusive in their actions. What I see now is a fearful person who is really seeking help but doesn't know how to ask for it. Seeing it this way isn't a huge adjustment to make in our thinking. My capacity to do it proves that. But the rewards of making this change in how we perceive the actions of others is well worth any effort we make. Not only are we more willing to be helpful, but the other person has a chance to change a harmful behavior too.

Today will quite likely give us an opportunity to observe an appeal for healing and help. The question is, how will we respond?

16.
Seek to know peace. Nothing more.

This sounds so simple, doesn't it? And it is pretty simple. But it can mean many things, depending on the seeker. What comes first to my mind is stillness. I empty my mind of the niggling thoughts that draw me from one scenario to another and just rest. In those moments of rest, peace pays a visit.

For others, peace may result from a daily meditation practice. Just paying a visit to the God within our minds promises peace too. We can only think of one thought at a time. If we are thinking about God, all else that might be nudging us into chaos will fall away.

Finally, peace is a decision: a choice to step away from encounters that are trying to ensnare our egos; to quiet our minds when chaos begins to reign; and to ask God, who is ever present, to help us in that moment of discontent. Peace will come regardless of which path we take.

If we want peace, it is ours. Now.

17.
My lifetime listens to yours.
—Muriel Rukeyser

This quote resonates so beautifully in my mind. In this journey we share with so many, our primary purpose is to be attentive to one another—attentive in a loving way. And one of the most loving things we will ever do is offer rapt attention to one another's words. It's one thing to hear each other, but quite another to actually listen. Listening is honoring one another's whole being.

Having someone truly be present for our life is an amazing gift. When another human is hearing our every word as it's uttered, it is a holy instant. Paying them that same respect is the gift repaid. The holiness of these exchanges can't be overestimated. They are intentional exchanges, because every person we encounter is on assignment to us. We are where we are right on cue.

What joy it can bring us to know that we will always be led to the right place at the right time. Always.

18.

**Love is the only sane and satisfactory answer
to the problem of human existence.
— Erich Fromm**

This idea encompasses so much. And because of my belief in it, it's one I have discussed from a number of vantage points in any number of meditations throughout this book. After forty-five years in recovery from addictions, I have come to believe that by far the most effective healing balm is offering ourselves in a loving way to help another person on this journey through life. Any problem one is faced with can be alleviated, at least a tiny bit, by the knowledge that someone else understands one's plight.

Love is expressed in myriad ways, of course. It can be as quiet as a smile or a bouquet of flowers. Gently resting a hand on someone's arm can be an expression of love between two friends. A kind note or an invitation to dinner is generally interpreted as a loving gesture too. And in each case, the person on the receiving end is being assured that all will be well in time. And generally, that's all any of us ever need to know.

The only thing we really need to do today, or any day, is be a comfort to those persons we encounter. They have paid us a visit for just that reason.

19.

Experiences mirror attitudes.

We have all heard that gratitude influences attitude. And many of us learned, perhaps years ago, that when we were feeling self-pity, anger, or overwhelming fear, making a gratitude list could quickly change how we might experience our lives in that moment. If we want a different experience, we have to do our part to cultivate a different attitude.

The good news is that changing our attitude isn't that difficult. It primarily grows out of a decision we make to take better control over our lives. And we do this by not allowing our minds to run amok. By changing our minds, we change our lives. And we change our minds one small step at a time.

For instance, giving up our judgments of others profoundly changes us—as well as our attitudes. Not only do we see them differently, but we see ourselves in a more loving light too. As I've said before, who (and what) we see mirrors ourselves. No one can change this but us.

Today will offer me many chances to experience my life in a more positive way.

20.
To let go means to stop—now!

How simple, yet profound. Letting go changes everything, for us and for whomever we are trying to control. To let go of others means letting all the folks in our life make their own choices, have their own opinions, and do whatever it is that's pulling at their own coattails. We need not be consulted. And unless we are asked, offering an opinion is quite unnecessary. In fact, it ought to be verboten.

Learning to keep quiet, to keep our thoughts to ourselves, to refrain from offering the "helpful" advice that screams within us to be shared, is the best gift we can give the friends and other loved ones who have chosen to share our path. What we may not realize until after we practice this suggestion for a while is that our lives are far less burdened when we let go and let others live as they choose. We free them, but we too are freed in the process.

To be free means letting others be free as well. Choosing only for ourselves today is a mighty gift—to everyone.

21.
If a thought is troubling you, choose another one.

That sounds so reasonable, doesn't it? Just choose another thought. And if one doesn't come quickly to mind, think about God instead. I actually love the simplicity of that idea; replace any unhelpful thought with the thought of God. You can think of God in any context: as a comforter, a listener, a guide, the One who always loves you. You don't need an image of Him at all. Just saying "God" quietly over and over is certain to release you from a troubling thought.

There is no doubt that we all experience many more troubling thoughts than positive, peaceful ones. That's evidence of how powerful the ego is. But we can decide to discard any one of those thoughts just as quickly as it comes if we have the willingness to let it go, replacing it with a fond memory, perhaps, or with the thought of God. Either way, we can maintain control of who and what we think about. And that's a powerful realization.

Today will afford me many opportunities to savor fond memories or thoughts of God. Either way, my day will be blessed.

22.
Relax, all is for the best.

This is not an easy idea to embrace when a major tragedy has occurred, for example, the death of a loved one or the loss of a job or a marriage. But most of us can understand in hindsight that the experience eventually moved us to a far different perspective. For instance, the unexpected death of a child often helps parents make the choice to begin a movement that ultimately helps hundreds of thousands of families experiencing a similar heartbreak.

The loss of my first marriage, which devastated me at the time, propelled me into a graduate program that hadn't been on my radar screen at all. And I've known so many people who have lost jobs only to discover they were being invited to enter a new door where a far better job awaited them.

Every experience is part of the perfect tapestry of our lives. We can see now, if we are willing, how past disappointments were actually the precursors to current blessings. And this kind of experience will be repeated again and again.

Embracing all that comes our way today is perfect and it releases us from all anguish. How easy life can be if we choose this perspective today.

23

Whoever is happy will make others happy too.
—Anne Frank

Happiness can be contagious. But someone has to go first. And even when others around us are happy, we can resist the choice to be happy. No doubt we have done just that hundreds of times. Why is it that we'd rather be aloof from God, angry, spiteful, or full of fear than give in to the happiness that is always God's gift in the moment?

When I look at my own life, I realize I spent years chasing happiness in all the wrong places. I failed to realize that aligning myself with God was the sure path to happiness and peace of mind. And as I have aged, I have come to equate the two absolutely.

When we stop and consider this quote came from Anne Frank, a young woman who really had very little to be happy about, we begin to understand that happiness is an inside job. You make the decision and then your decision serves as an example to others that they can make that choice too, if it suits them.

With God as my guide, I'll choose to be happy today. My example might help others too.

24.

If you keep saying things are going to be bad, you have a good chance of being a prophet.
—Isaac B. Singer

We have unmistakable power to determine what kind of day we are going to have. And when we have assumed a particular experience is going to be bad, we quite knowingly see all the negative aspects as they present themselves. Of course, there always are some. And we dismiss all the positive aspects in the process. Of course, there are always just as many of those. We end up with exactly what we have decided to experience. We are solely responsible.

We have to want a different kind of life if we are ever to have one. No one has the power to choose our thoughts or make our assumptions for us. That's the good news. And if you have decided you want a more peaceful, productive life, be extremely careful in the choices you are making. What you get will reflect your choices.

Today is uncharted. But each one of us has the power to determine, at the close of the day, if it was a good one or a bad one.

25.
Forgiveness is the touchstone to peace of mind.

Why is forgiveness so central to our lives? The answer isn't that hard to discern. We spend much of every day sitting in judgment of the people who are crossing our paths; much of the time, it's at an unconscious level. But it's happening, regardless. And when we allow the ego that much control over our lives, not very much of any day feels peaceful.

But there is a solution to this lack of peace. And it lies within our willingness to forgive ourselves for our judgments of others. Of course, this has to be coupled with our willingness to forgive the imagined slights we think others have committed against us. Never forget, *we are always seeing what we choose to see.* And it's really ourselves we are seeing in that moment of judgment of others. This idea may not be easy to grasp, but it's true nonetheless. The sooner we accept it, the more quickly we will be able to change how we see all that's unfolding before us.

May I be willing to see all others through the eyes of love today. And if I forget for a moment, may I be willing to forgive myself and see anew.

26.
This too shall pass.
—Eleanor Roosevelt

No doubt this idea has been attributed to many people. And Mrs. Roosevelt might not have been the first to say it. But its real value is what's important here, not who said it or when. It's an idea that allows us to relax, to trust that the passage of time changes how everything looks and feels.

When I first heard this phrase in recovery rooms, I didn't grasp it. I didn't understand that it was possible to simply let things go. I didn't have a relationship with a Higher Power at that time, so to turn to Him for help was a very foreign idea. Now I rely on that Power completely. I know that whatever is happening is offering me a lesson, an opportunity that I'm ready for; and that it will visit for only as long as need be. And then it will pass.

This four-word phrase, "This too shall pass," is the kindest solution to any troubling situation in our lives. Nothing sticks around for any longer than is needed for our "education."

27.
It takes a lot of courage to allow ourselves to be vulnerable, to be soft.
—Dudley Martineau

After making the choice to be soft the first time, it becomes an easier choice from then on—markedly easier. And being a softer role model for others serves such a good purpose. It allows others to see that vulnerability is a good thing. We need be neither tough nor domineering to be courageous. Being soft is far more courageous and is ultimately contagious, too.

The big payoff of being soft, however, is that it promotes peace between all people, even adversaries. It's far harder to respond in a critical way to someone who has just shown you their vulnerable side. In fact, we are far more likely to be vulnerable in return. Can you imagine, just for a moment, what our world might look like if we were all responding to one another in a soft, kind way? There could be a major shift in the universe. What a glorious thought.

We will all have many opportunities today to be part of the shift toward gentleness in all responses. Committing to the first one will make each consecutive one easier.

28.
Discipline is the basis of a satisfying life.
—Katharine Hepburn

Being committed to our goals, whatever they may be, ushers in a feeling of accomplishment, of healthy pride. We know, all too well, what it feels like to make a list of what we intend to do and then push the list aside, day after day. But there are many ways to be disciplined, and they don't all add up to just checking off what's on our list. We can be disciplined about how we treat the others sharing this path we are on. For instance, we can make sure we are always cordial and helpful in even a small way if possible.

The first line of one of my favorite prayers is: "I am here only to be truly helpful." Keeping that in mind in a disciplined way as I pass by others on the street or at the grocery means I will not only feel a sense of satisfaction, I will make it possible for others to feel appreciated too.

Today stands before us just awaiting our actions. What we do is always our choice. Let's make it satisfying to others, as well as ourselves.

29.
Each moment is unique and will never come again.

We know this implicitly, don't we? Yet we spend most of our moments someplace other than here and now. The past pulls many of us down the proverbial rabbit hole, sometimes for hours or even days at a time. And our fears about the future can completely steal the only real life we have, which is here, right now. There is only one path to peace, and it's a simple one. Look into this moment and be glad.

There is nothing magical about claiming this moment for all it's worth. It takes a decision, first and foremost. And then it takes the willingness to practice living this moment only. How do we get from where we are to this way of living? We seek to be aware of God. He is fully a part of every moment we are given. Feel God's presence and you know *now*. It's just that simple.

God and now are one—just as God and we are one. Sink into this truth and you will be at peace.

30.
Let each look to himself and see what God wants of him and attend to this, leaving all else alone.
—Henry Suso

Doing that which we think God wants us to do, and nothing else, is not such a difficult assignment. We may think we don't know what that assignment is, but that's primarily because we have chosen to complicate what it may be. I have decided to keep my assignment very simple: be helpful, in every instance and with each person. Period!

We can make ourselves crazy trying to figure out a more complicated assignment. I know—I did that for many years when I first committed myself to a spiritual pathway. But in time, I realized it's the obvious thing that presents itself which is the real task. Knowing, as I now do, that those people who cross my path are there specifically for me to help makes my life far more manageable and peaceful too. Indeed, that assignment ends up helping me as much as those I help.

Wherever we travel today, and whomever we encounter, is part of the perfect plan we are fulfilling at this moment in time. The next perfect part is to be kind.

31.

Time spent attempting to change others affords little time for personal change.
—Georgette Vickstrom

Oh, my goodness. The hours most of us have spent trying to change others would fill many calendars of appointments. And it was all for naught. We very simply cannot change others! Period. We just can't, no matter how clever we make the request or the demand. We can cajole, plead, threaten, or withhold favors. We can punish, but we can't force someone against his or her will to change a behavior or an opinion that doesn't sit well with us.

In all honesty, we are extremely lucky that we aren't burdened with being in charge of everyone's behavior or opinions. If we were tasked with this job, we'd be exhausted all of the time and unendingly disappointed. Being in charge of ourselves is a big enough job for us to handle, and there are many challenges that each one of us could profit from addressing. The decision to give up control is at the top of the list for anyone who wants to experience what peace feels like.

Being in charge of our own behavior today is a big enough job. And it's one each one of us can handle with the help of our Higher Power.

APRIL

1.

**I guess I am ready, or I never would have
started down this rocky road.
—Jill Clark**

I have grown into the belief that whatever comes down the road
toward us is an experience we have agreed to grow through. And
that idea can allow all of us to be willing to embrace life as it is,
knowing that there is good that can result from every experience,
regardless of what it is. We may not see it immediately; however, in
all cases, if we are willing, we will see it and be willing to embrace it
in hindsight.

Hindsight does indeed clarify so many things in one's life. Just take
a moment and think about the last year of your life. Each one of us
had a host of experiences that baffled us, scared us, or unexpectedly
thrilled us. And we had no advance knowledge that even one of
those specific experiences was headed our way. But the experience
came because we were ready. And our readiness meant we could
become guides along the way for others too. No experience is
solely for us.

*What a glorious realization that what we get serves many others too. Our
acceptance is the first step to becoming who we were born to be.*

2.

**The greatest happiness you can have is knowing
that you do not necessarily require happiness.
—William Saroyan**

What does it actually mean to be happy when happiness can be
described in so many ways? To some, happiness is equated with joy.
To others, happiness is peace of mind. And to still others, happiness
is acceptance of things as they are. The idea of surrendering to
circumstances, rather than always fighting with them, allows for a
sense of relief that can be compared to happiness by many.

Happiness obviously isn't just one thing. And knowing that, as Saroyan says, *just being* is quite good enough allows for a sustained kind of happiness to which we can lay claim by making a simple decision.

Acceptance of life as it presents itself, believing that it is unfolding as "has been scripted," is quite possibly the shortest pathway to happiness, and it's a journey that every one of us is invited to make every day. All it takes is a decision.

Do you really want happiness? If yes, the road there is open now.

3.

Unexpected experiences are the gifts we have been waiting for.

I heard a friend say some years ago that unexpected experiences were dancing lessons from God. I always loved that expression, probably because it runs counter to the more common idea that when something unexpected happens, it's usually not good.

As I have aged, I've decided to live with more acceptance. It's just too hard to try to bend every experience to my definition of what's good. In the process of changing my perspective, I have discovered that most experiences are, indeed, quite good. And some of them are even exceptional.

Our experiences will directly reflect our interpretation of each one. Thus, we will be opening gifts all day if that's our choice.

Claiming responsibility for how this day before you unfolds is, in itself, the gift you have been waiting for.

4.

Courage is the price that life exacts for granting peace.
—Amelia Earhart

In May of 2020, millions of people worldwide protested the murder of George Floyd, whose name will go down in history as the Black man whose death at the hands of law enforcement catalyzed long-needed change throughout the world. I think it's extremely courageous of those who have dared to confront racism, which is not just endemic in the United States, but in other countries too. It's never too late to stand up for what is right. It is *never* too late.

But courage is often in short supply, and there are many reasons for that. Many of us grew up in families where standing up for our beliefs resulted in rejection by our family members or friends. Being courageous enough to speak our mind isn't easy, particularly not when our words ring hollow to those who are standing close by. But not sharing our own truth means that peace can never be experienced. Peace and truth go hand in hand. Being fully transparent is the price that must be paid for peace of mind. And it's a price worth paying.

May we each be courageous enough today to be truthful and loving, at the same time. Then peace will be ours.

5.

God allows us to experience the low points of life in order to teach us lessons we could not learn in any other way.
—C. S. Lewis

Note that Lewis says God "allows us" to experience these low points. He doesn't say that God *causes* the low points. And that's a crucially important distinction. We come into this life to learn a host of lessons, and those people we encounter on our journey have been selected to experience certain lessons right along with us. That's the beauty of the journey we share. It's about a process of give-and-take. It's about being a teacher as well as a student. It's about knowing we need each other to become all that we each are destined to be.

Perhaps the most interesting aspect of a low point is that it generally turns out to be one of the more enlightening of all our experiences. Certainly hindsight has revealed on many occasions that when I was sure all was lost, I was actually on my way to being "found." Recovery from alcoholism is just one of many examples of this. The journey is always as it needs to be. Peace is the gift we get when we accept this as truth.

All is well. All is always well. Peace resides in the acceptance of this. Let's remember this today.

6.

I have a simple philosophy. Fill what's empty.
Empty what's full. And scratch where it itches.
—Alice Roosevelt Longworth

It's so easy to complicate our lives unnecessarily. Making the decision to look only at what lies before us and solely dealing with that would change our lives immensely. Peace is surely a long shot for those of us who live in tomorrow. Unfortunately, that's where most of us live a good percentage of the time.

Coming to believe that each one of us has a Higher Power who has tomorrow in His sights allows us to focus our attention on what lies before us in this single moment. What a difference this makes in our state of mind. Keeping our focus on here and now lessens the angst that living in the future so often triggers. Making the choice to live only here and now truly simplifies our lives and makes all decisions far more manageable. Nothing can baffle us for long if we can only stay in this moment.

Stepping back from tomorrow changes everything. With practice, we can change our lives forever.

7.

Letting others walk their own path is the surest
way to freedom and peace of mind.

It's far too easy to think that those who travel with us are in need of our direction, whether couched as "helpfulness" or offered as an obvious criticism. Those who walk beside us need our acceptance and love. Period. They come as our teachers and as our students. It's from and through them that we learn who we are and who we can become. No one will enter our circle of associates who doesn't have a particular reason for being there—nary a one.

Accepting this as the truth of our lives allows us to look at each person and every moment from a fresh perspective. Many of us grew up in families where outsiders were often suspect. Our families may have been insular, seemingly not aware that others traveling among us come as friends and teachers. They may have been seen as interlopers in one way or another. But we have now learned how wrong that interpretation was. We are a community of students, all clearly in need of one another's tutelage; knowing that offers us the peace we long for.

If we want to experience peace, there is one way to find it. Let go of those who travel with us. Just let go.

8.

Without solitude, I get dull, like a bird without a song.
—Abby Warman

Quiet time for many of us is when we collect ourselves. It's when we connect with the inner voice who has the answers we seek. It's also when we find out who we really are. The question that might well be uppermost in our minds during our moments of solitude is, "Am I showing up in this life the way I truly want to?" In the silence, we find that answer. In the silence, we come face to face with ourselves.

How fortunate those of us are who practice prayer and meditation on a regular basis. It really is what feeds one's soul and assures us of the *Presence* that has never left our side. And the great blessing is that we don't even have to be aware of the *Presence* for it to be there. It simply never leaves. It waits, knowing that at some point we will be inspired to seek its wisdom.

Will today be the day we seek the wisdom of the Presence that's always with us? It will wait until that moment comes —whenever it is.

9.

**When we loosen our grasp on our concerns, there
is room for the spiritual essence of all life to move
through us in such a way that healing occurs.**
— Carol Sheffield

Loosening our grasp on our concerns is another way of saying
"letting go" of them. And when we actually let go of the behavior
of any person or the outcome of any situation, we discover an
immediate feeling of relief, the kind of relief that softly says, "God is
here to handle this." And that moment of relief is where our healing
lies in every instance. Why do we so often resist God's help? Is it
because our ego strives so hard to control?

Fortunately, God holds no grudges. He allows for all of our
decisions. His help will be available whenever we choose to avail
ourselves of it. It will remain in the wings until we are willing to say,
"Yes, I see now what I need to do." But the ego holds us hostage
for just as long as we allow it to. And the more we resist letting go,
the greater becomes its intent to take charge. The good news is that
the tighter it holds on, the more willing we eventually become to see
that there is another way.

*Seeing another way is what makes all the difference in whether we have a
trying life or a peaceful one. This choice is constantly before us.*

10.

**Too many things in today's rushed and hurried
world seem to require immediate attention.**
— Karen Davis

Does everything need immediate attention? I think not. In fact,
I'd dare to say that almost nothing needs immediate attention,
particularly if you eliminate incidents involving children or the
elderly. For sure, a fire needs to be addressed right now. And so
does a call for help. But how often do these kinds of occurrences
happen? And when we stand back and assess what needs to be
done in virtually any situation that has called out to us, we can see
that there's time to make a studied and calm response.

I think it becomes habitual to think we need to address everything immediately. And too often, immediate responses are not carefully thought out. Taking a few deep breaths before making any response will allow for clarity and the more measured response. We will experience few peaceful moments in our lives if we are always ready to jump into action without first taking the time to evaluate what's really needed.

Today may well offer me a chance to be quite measured in a response. I pray for clarity and peace of mind as I make my decision.

11.

The simple act of offering comfort changes the moment in unimaginable ways.

What a beautiful thought this is. And the very act of comforting someone else comforts us too. Being a comfort in the lives of others can perhaps be considered our most holy of all "assignments" in this experience that we share with so many intentional visitors on our path. Nary a one has come our way accidentally. And each person needs our love and acceptance, both of which may serve to comfort them.

I'm not implying that every person we meet is going to be easy to love or accept, but by the very nature of the fact that they have shown up, we know they have been sent and that we need them as much as they need us. Every time we extend the hand of love, our own lives are healed a tiny bit more. What we give does indeed come back to us.

May I be fully aware, each moment today, that my expressions of love are what's called for.

12.

Give up arguing, one argument at a time.

How much more peaceful our lives would be if we paused before engaging in an unnecessary disagreement. And every disagreement is, after all, unnecessary. It's only the overactive ego that thinks disagreements are important. The ego keeps us constantly engaged with conflict, thus, it is constantly relishing the fact that it has usurped control of our lives. Every time we give into an argument, we are giving the ego power.

Fortunately, there is a far better way to navigate daily life. And we know what it is: Walk with quiet intention. Speak from a place of love. Allow all the people we meet to feel the hand of love that we are offering. Step aside when invited to engage in a negative way with others. Let everyone be who he has decided to be in the moment, maintaining our own resolve to be a peaceful traveler every step of our journey.

I will not be seduced into an argument with anyone today. The only winners are those who choose to turn the other cheek.

13.
You have to feel that you make a difference.
— Monty Cralley

Making a difference in the lives of others might not be a priority for everyone. But my own life has shown me that when I lead from a place of love in even the most ordinary exchanges with others, it makes a difference in my own life, and perhaps that's the only one we can be certain of ever affecting.

However, I have come to believe that even *wanting* to have a positive impact on the lives of others is a game changer. For many, it might mean one's demeanor has changed. Or it might mean the willingness to be helpful has moved to center stage. For others, it might demonstrate that life in the future need not mimic life as it was, and this can have far-reaching consequences.

Deciding to be an example of kindness, love, or helpfulness makes clear just what we need to do in each next moment. How much simpler life can be when we decide to choose among these three options.

The opportunity to have a positive impact every time we encounter another person — whether a friend or a stranger — is a constant occurrence. The question is: do we take that opportunity?

———————— 14. ————————

Being self-absorbed is frighteningly common and doesn't bode well for the well-being of society.

How fitting this sentiment is for far too many of us. Thinking of ourselves first is perhaps endemic. But it doesn't have to be the full truth of our lives. The good news is that the ego can learn. We can decide to see others more compassionately, and this decision will change us. And change we must if we want to be helpful fellow travelers on this planet.

It's absolutely never too late to begin behaving differently toward the others we wander among. Being aware of how we want to be known and remembered by them is an opportunity in every moment. In each conversation with someone else, we are revealing who we are. Are we pleased with the "presentation"? If not, we know what to do. Indeed, we do know what to do, and the time to do it is now.

There is no greater gift we can offer humankind than a helpful hand. Will you do your part today?

———————— 15. ————————

Chaos is not a magnet.

It is a common response, an all-too-common one in fact, to be engaged by chaos — any form of chaos. Why does it ensnare us so easily? Some would say it's because the ego is always looking for a "rumble" of sorts. And any of us who has struggled with the ego, which always seeks to be right, understands how easily this can happen. Getting sucked into an altercation of any kind can be seductive. But it doesn't have to reel us in — no, it doesn't. We are responsible for every choice we make to get involved.

Knowing that we are in the seat of power and that no one makes any choice for us can also become seductive in its own way. Being fully aware and in charge of who we are every moment is an awesome responsibility for sure, but it's one we have been prepared for.

We can rejoice about being who we really want to be in the many encounters we experience on a daily basis. This can be an assignment we relish. And when we show up peacefully, we will be a magnet of a far finer kind.

Today stands before us like an open book. The choice we make in every situation writes the story of who we are this day. Let's be satisfied with how the story ends.

16.

The game of life is a game of boomerangs. Our thoughts, deeds, and words return to us sooner or later, with astounding accuracy. — Florence Scovel Shinn

The idea that what we give to others always returns to us should make each one of us a bit circumspect before we take any action or offer any words of advice to our fellow travelers. This is not a childish game we are playing. And we'd better consider very carefully what it is we want from life so that we can make that our own offering to life. The scales will be balanced. We must first lay our best on the scales if we want the best to return to us. It's not a difficult equation.

Upon arising each morning, we can set an intention for what we want to give and then receive throughout the day. We have far more control of how our activities unfold then we may have assumed. While it's true we will never be able to control the actions of others, we can perhaps modify them by how we choose to "play our hand." Let's never doubt the rewards of kindness. Remember, what we give will come back to us.

Today lies before us fresh and unblemished by any actions. With God's help, we can paint the day beautiful, both for ourselves and others.

17.

What we think determines what we see.
—Jane Nelson

The power of our thoughts is awesome, no doubt far greater than
most of us ever realize. Some spiritual philosophies espouse the
idea that every thought manifests somewhere, and I'm inclined to
agree. What I choose to see "out here" is what unfolds before my
eyes. If I want a different experience of life, it's up to me to create a
different picture.

Of course, this means I'm responsible for every experience I have.
Some may think this idea leaves too little wiggle room for the
unexpected; but those who are adherents of this idea would say,
"There is nothing unexpected that ever happens." This sounds
pretty dramatic, but it's actually extremely sensible. If you take
responsibility for your thoughts, you can be pretty certain that your
life will be just as you chart it. And that removes the anxiety from
our lives. What could be better than that?

*Knowing that we are the creators of how our lives unfold keeps us on our
toes. The wandering mind can take us where we don't really want to go. Stay
alert today.*

18.

To speak ill of others is a dishonest way of praising ourselves.
—Will Durant

I have to admit I have been guilty of this behavior. And I'm certainly
not proud of it. I doubt that I'm the only one among us who needs to
plead guilty. But who we were is not who we have to continue being.
And that's something to be eternally grateful for. *We can change.* I have
made many changes over the years. Every good change I have made
has led me to a better frame of mind, to a better experience with
others, and to a better position in how my life is moving forward.

Admitting our faults, though sometimes humiliating, is actually
the only way we can feel free. It's the only way we can look in the
mirror and feel proud of who we are becoming. And it's the only

way we can confidently navigate the journey that we are making. Carrying baggage from the past around who we were prevents us from opening the door to who we are meant to be now.

Opportunities to let go of guilt and old behaviors come to us regularly. Today doesn't have to end like it began.

19.

I wonder what my life would be like if I were to focus my energy and thoughts only on things that really matter.
—Robbie Dircks

That thought is one worth mulling over. No doubt many of us spend multiple hours a day allowing our minds to wander into unproductive territory. Coupled with all the wasted hours spent trying to control people and situations where failure is the norm, it adds up to hours of frustration for most of us. But we don't have to live this way forever. We can proactively choose to place our energies and our thoughts where they will reap benefits for ourselves and others.

How lucky we are that no one but ourselves is in charge of who we become in any situation. Even when we want to blame someone else, which is not uncommon, we must finally accept responsibility for what we have created. And the plus is that only we can change whatever we have wrought. Power is something we have, just not over others. And that's what really matters.

Moving into today with an intention to mind my business and spend my energies in productive ways will ensure at least a modicum of peace, and that's far better than no peace at all.

20.

The truth is that you always know the right thing to do. The hard part is doing it.
—Venugopal Acharya

There is a place within each of us that always knows what's right. We can block this knowledge, of course. And our egos are generally at work doing just that. But there is the softer voice of one's Higher Power that wants to direct all of our thoughts and actions for the good of humanity. And the more we turn to that voice for guidance, the greater is our peace of mind.

The additional payoff of turning to the softer voice is that it begins to change us in ways we hadn't expected. We become kinder, more helpful people, and the habit of kindness becomes ingrained in us. Everyone whose path we cross benefits when we listen to that voice, and of course, we benefit too. When we help others, we help ourselves and our world changes.

We will have many opportunities today to effect helpful changes for the people we encounter. Our only assignment is to listen to the voice of our Higher Power.

21.
Believe the best in yourself. Then it is easier to believe the best in others.
—Mardy Kopischki

It is said that who we see is who we are in that moment. We project ourselves onto others. This was not an idea I easily embraced when I was first introduced to it. I didn't want to accept that the negative assessments I so often made of others really reflected my own qualities, thrust on to them. Surely these were not *my* qualities! But too many wise folks said otherwise, and I began to lower my resistance to this initially unappreciated truth. And then so much became clear to me.

Seeing ourselves in others allows us to see firsthand what we may want to change in ourselves. It's like taking a shortcut to self-improvement. I don't mean to imply that it's easy to embrace these qualities in ourselves, but we can embrace how seeing them "over there" allows us to more easily change them "here." We are each a work in progress. And there is nothing wrong with that. It's progress, not perfection, that we are striving for.

We will likely be confronted with people today who have something to reveal to us about ourselves. And that's good. All change begins there.

22.

**To show great love for God and our neighbor,
we need not do great things.**
— Mother Teresa

It's nice to be reminded that living an ordinary life with simple
kindness in our hearts is quite enough to make this a better world.
Mother Teresa did do great things, but, in her heart, she felt she
was just doing what God had called her to do. We are all being
called by God to do something specific, something that can't be
done by anyone else in the way we can do it. And few of us are
called to do something extraordinary. Just being among the human
race with love in our hearts is the most common of all callings. And
that's not beyond the capability of any one of us.

Making the decision to live a simple life, showing kindness and
respect for others, will please God. We are assured of that. And we
really need do very little more. If every one of us did one kind thing
every day, the universe would shift for the better.

*Making the choice to do one kind thing today will feel good, and it will please
others too. Not really a hard choice, is it?*

23.

**When it comes time to do your own life, you
either perpetuate your childhood or you stand
on it and finally kick it out from under.**
— Rosellen Brown

What does it mean to kick our past aside? I interpret it as meaning
we want to live now, not reliving the past over and over. I think too
many therapists encourage folks to stay in the past for far too long.
It's certainly not that it hasn't played a significant role in who we
are in the present; it has, for sure. But real healing ultimately relies
on our staying focused on this moment. It's in this moment that we
find God's presence, and it's that presence that ultimately heals us.

We all know people who can't seem to move beyond the past.
Sometimes it might be fond memories of the past that claim their

attention, but more commonly it's the hurts that continue to hold them hostage. The result of this is that these folks are missing the gifts that are being offered, right here, right now. Our own example of choosing a different way to navigate this journey, for example, by choosing to relish life moment by moment, may be the encouragement needed by one of our fellow travelers.

Living solely in the present, letting the past be done with us, gives us a far different life experience—one that may be exemplary.

24.
All is pattern, all life, but we can't always see the pattern when we're part of it.
—Belva Plain

Hindsight is a gift that enlightens us as we journey through life. Seldom do we see, in the midst of an experience, just how it is adding a necessary thread to the tapestry our lives are weaving. But we can be certain that no experience is superfluous to the destination, the final picture, we are heading for. Growing accustomed to the truth of this gives us peace of mind. And peace of mind is what we all are so deserving of.

What a blessing to know that no experience is meant to throw us off course. We may not understand its purpose while wandering through it, but we can be confident that there is one. And we can be equally confident that we will understand its value to our journey before arriving at our destination.

What joy we can claim when we allow ourselves the fuller view of our experiences? Nary a one of them came unbidden.

Let's never forget that God is in the midst of every experience we will meet along the path today.

———— 25. ————

Each friend represents a world in us, a world
possibly not born until they arrive.
—Anais Nin

The assurance that we will meet exactly who we need to meet is a hopeful one. We need not wonder why someone has shown up on our path. All we need to embrace is that those who do manifest in our lives have a specific purpose for joining our journey. Each and every one of them will call out in us a quality that we will either embrace or abhor. In either case, it's part of the education we need to become the person we agreed to be in this life.

That we don't immediately understand why someone has suddenly appeared on our horizon isn't a cause for alarm. They came because they must. We encountered them because we must. There are no unintentional visitors on our journey. Each one is offering us a "gift" we need in order to move on to the next level of our progress as men and women in this experience called life. Each encounter is perfect for the two of us.

Choosing to be grateful for every encounter we have is the assurance that we will be learning what we need to learn today. What an easy decision this is.

———— 26. ————

The man who views his world at fifty the same as he
did at twenty has wasted thirty years of his life.
—Muhammad Ali

Living in the past can be seductive, particularly if one's past was a successful one. However, every moment is offering us exactly what we need right now, so if we aren't attuned to this moment, we are missing the "education" we need to make progress on our journey. There is nothing complicated about this principle. It's a choice we must make moment by moment to embrace the gift God is offering us in the present. The gifts never quit coming. That's the promise He makes us.

Living in yesterday is far too easy. Even if yesterday wasn't a time of success, we can still get ensnared in the same way a toothache prevents us from moving forward. There is only the ever present *now* if we want to live within the opportunities that are slated to come our way. It's understandable that some people want to stay in the past because it brought them either great joy or pain; however, staying there means no additional joys will ever bless their journey.

This day beckons us with the perfect opportunities we need for the many tomorrows in our life. Let's not turn our back on them.

27.
The bottom line is I am responsible for my own well-being, my own happiness.
—Kathleen Andrus

We are powerless over so many things in our life; for instance, we can't control any other person who crosses our path, nor the outcomes of the many situations we encounter. However, we are never powerless over how we perceive our experiences and all the choices that are available to us. In fact, being empowered in every instance to make the choices that seem right and good for us and our fellow men is being in charge of quite a lot. Not having any other responsibility offers us much deserved freedom to live from our hearts with every choice that we do make.

Being grateful for our limited power is refreshing and mind-altering. We mistakenly think that controlling others is what would bring us happiness, but quite the opposite is true. Having that kind of power would deplete our energies very quickly and our peace of mind instantly. Being responsible for ourselves is the way to all the happiness we feel we deserve.

Claim all the happiness you desire by looking to this day with intention.

EACH DAY A RENEWED BEGINNING

28.

Taking a time-out will benefit everyone.

We generally think of a time-out as a way to reprimand children when they are acting out. However, we adults can benefit from mini time-outs too; not because we have acted out but simply because we need to quietly regroup and remember why we are here and how to open our hearts.

A time-out can be used for making a gratitude list, which never fails to change our mindset. A time-out can give us a few moments to quietly meditate or have a chat with God. Or maybe we just need to take a ten-minute nap. Time away from the world blesses us in myriad ways.

Perhaps the more important reason for a time-out, however, is that during our time-out, we allow the others in our lives to enjoy the freedom to live without our interference. We rest, and they live freely. It's a win-win situation.

Any time we feel stressed out or overwhelmed, it's time for a time-out, one that will give us the moments of freedom we deserve to live peacefully.

29.

The ordinary human being thinks about
twelve thousand thoughts a day.
—Susan Smith Jones

Our minds are seldom quiet. During those moments devoted to meditation, they are generally still, but even in prayer, aren't we sending thoughts God's way? It's not that thinking is bad; on the contrary, but we all need time to just be—time without the ordinary clutter in our minds, time to relish the gift of a peaceful mind. And it's not really possible to have a peaceful mind if thoughts are racing through it, even if those thoughts are happy ones.

I don't mean to disparage thinking. Without the thinking minds of great scientists, researchers, and philosophers, our universe would be in desperate straits. However, there's a decided difference between thoughts that further humankind and thoughts that destroy our individual and collective humanity. Even the greatest of all thinkers needs moments of stillness.

Moments of silence might well offer the solutions that escape us when chatter fills our minds. For sure, moments of silence will offer us respite from the noise of living.

Let's take time away from all noise today and be still. Simply be still.

30.

Each of us is the pupil of whichever one of us could best teach what each of us needed to learn.
—Maria Isabel Barreno

We can count on our teachers showing up. And that's one of the undeniable absolutes in our lives. As has already been said, we are always serving in the capacity of helpmates to one another. In fact, that's the very reason we have encountered each other. There are no interlopers on our path. We each showed up for a specific reason, and we each will play the role we have heretofore agreed to play.

Wandering through life with this belief system undergirding us surely makes our journey more understandable, as well as more manageable. We don't have to fret about a certain encounter we had. We can accept that it was meant for our education. And when we meet up with someone we had dreaded seeing, it helps to know that that meeting was purposeful as well. Whatever comes is right on schedule. Whoever comes is specific to our needs.

What a relief if we embrace this idea. Everyone has been called to make our journey complete.

MAY

1.

Our greatest lesson in life may be to keep it simple.

One of life's many conundrums is our ill-considered attraction to making it more complicated than it needs to be. Is it that we can't believe simpler ways of navigating life are the best? Or are we just drawn to the more complex, believing that we are far too sophisticated for the simpler, more sensible, or easier way? It probably doesn't matter which answer fits for us. Both are wrong. Keeping life simple just makes sense.

This is akin to deciding which fork in the road to take. The more obvious one is generally the best one. Our lives can be so much easier than we tend to make them. And this doesn't mean that our lives have any less value. That doesn't play into it at all. It just means that we generally can't believe that the easiest path through life is the best path. Perhaps we should try specifically choosing the simpler way for a while and see what results.

Today will undoubtedly offer a few opportunities to choose between a simple solution and a more complicated one. Let's try the simple one today.

2.

Life is like an unbridled horse.
—Kay Lovatt

The image of an unbridled horse is a joyful one. He frolics and jumps and runs from fence to fence. And he generally resists being saddled, at least at first. But then he settles into partnering up with his owner, knowing that he can trust her to guide him around the ring.

This image puts me in mind of how we may mentally or emotionally run from pillar to post sometimes as we try to figure out what our next best move might be, and then our companion, the God of our understanding, makes His presence known, and we settle down, trusting that there is a way to smoothly step forward.

We don't have to give up our freedom when we rely on God. We can choose not to rely on Him, as a matter of fact. But if we turn to Him, He will help us navigate the roadblocks as we gingerly move toward our goal. We are both free and guided at the same time. We have the best of both worlds.

An opportunity to rely on the God of our understanding will surely present itself today. Will we take it or turn away? How peaceful we are afterwards will reveal the choice we have made.

3.

We can't control others, no matter how hard we try or how right we think we are.

This idea may well disappoint us. It's not unusual to get invested in having people live the way we want them to live. Likewise, we want outcomes to match our picture of what they should be. Does this make us bad people? On the contrary; it makes us quite ordinary people, who like so many others traveling with us can fall into habitual tendencies and patterns. The underlying opportunity here is that *we can change*, even though we can't ever change anyone else. And that's beneficial, not only for us, but for everyone else who is trying to sort out their own lives.

There isn't anything we experience that can't be a learning opportunity, and giving up control just might be one of the most significant of them all. At first, we may likely feel great disappointment. However, as we grow accustomed to letting others be, we arrive at an understanding of how much more peaceful our own lives have become.

Choosing to be peaceful today is easy. Every time we let our friends or family members make their own choices, we will get a taste of it.

4.

**When you least expect it is when you are
overwhelmed with the generosity of others.**
—Iris Timberlake

To be blessed by another's generosity is one of the greatest gifts we
can receive. Let's not forget that generosity is good for the giver
too. It's the very definition of a win-win situation. Being a loving
presence in someone else's life is one sure way of changing the
vibration throughout the universe, the vibration that nurtures a
multitude of examples of love.

Many spiritual teachers believe that what we do for one is actually
felt by many because of the tendency to "pay it forward." So the
more we focus on offering random acts of kindness, the greater
will be our impact on our communities and the world beyond. An
unexpected payback is that our own lives are vastly improved by
each act of kindness. What we give does come back to us, in some
form, in time.

Being a generous soul simply feels right and good. And the
difference it makes to and within everyone cannot be overestimated.

*Every encounter today is an opportunity to offer a random act of kindness.
What a beautiful day we can be part of if we participate in this way.*

5.

**Listening means an unhurried time when God really can
have a chance to imprint his thoughts in your mind.**
—Frank N. D. Buchman

Most of us probably think we are pretty good listeners, even
though actually, the opposite is generally true. When it comes to
conversations with friends, family members, or even colleagues,
how often are we searching our minds for the perfect response even
before our companion has quit talking? This doesn't make us bad
people. In fact, it's a quite ordinary condition that most of us suffer
from. Staying intently focused on the conversation at hand is not

such an easy task and too often we are guilty of the same inattention when in "conversation" with God.

Prayer and meditation are extremely important practices for multitudes of people, but even for the most committed practitioners, being constantly focused on a message from God in our times of meditation is elusive. We may start out with great intentions, but then those fleeting thoughts about last night or what might happen this evening steal us away from God. Does He mind? Not really, but we are cheating ourselves every time we let yesterday or tomorrow take center stage when God is at hand.

We cannot do more than one thing at a time. If it's time to listen to God, we must put all else aside.

6.

Shifting perceptions changes us completely.

There are so many simple tools or shortcuts for helping us navigate more peacefully through this life we have chosen to experience, but from my perspective, none is more helpful than asking the God of my understanding to help me see a situation differently. I became familiar with this tool as a student of *A Course in Miracles*, which is a spiritual pathway that promotes making a commitment to always seeing and acting from a place of love.

Like with any new tool, I was a bit suspicious at first that the teachings didn't have the power to change me in any significant way. How wrong I was. Everything changes in the moment when we seek another way of seeing a situation. Initially I wondered how it could work so effectively and immediately; however, what I hadn't considered was the power of surrendering our ego in the very act of seeking a new vision. That surrender is what invites God in. And in that surrender, everything changes.

The opportunity to see anew is immensely powerful. And it's available to us any time we seek it.

7.

All that is necessary to make this world a better place to live is to love.
—Isadora Duncan

This suggestion sounds so simple on first hearing it. But how many of us are guided by the idea of actually loving all the people we encounter on a minute-by-minute basis? It's my guess that's not the first thing that comes to most minds when wandering the planet. And yet, how difficult would it be to make the decision to be a constant example of love as we maneuver through the day? It would take a decision. And it would take adherence to it. But the rest is just practice. Do unto others that which you hope others will do unto you.

Life would actually be far easier to live if once and for all, we made the decision to always be loving. We wouldn't have to stop and consider what we want to do in a certain situation. The decision would already have been made. And everyone benefits from our loving presence, not least ourselves.

Being a benefit to the whole human race is not so very hard. It begins with a simple decision. Are you willing to make it today?

8.

There is no area of personal challenge in your life that God's love cannot solve.
—Mary Kupferle

What a gift we have been given unbidden. We have God's love to support us, to comfort us, to guide us in every situation we will ever experience—every one of them! And we didn't have to do a thing to receive this gift; it is simply ours. Unfortunately, we don't always accept His gifts. We think we know better than God and we not only waste time, but hurt ourselves and others in the process.

We will all experience personal challenges—many of them. Some periods of our lives may seem to be more challenged than others, in fact. But God is always available to ease the pain of every challenge, and, even better, to guide us through or around the challenge. We will never be left high and dry. What lucky people we are. Our challenges are the opportunities we need to allow God to reveal to us just how present He is. Why don't we let Him go to work on our behalf?

We truly don't have a care in the world. God has all seeming problems under His care. We can coast. And trust.

9.
God sends no one away empty except those who are full of themselves.
—Dwight L. Moody

This quote made me laugh. We have all met people who are full of themselves. I met one the other day, in fact; a doctor I went to see about a medical condition. But I think there's a perfectly good explanation for the men and women who appear full of themselves. I think what's undergirding their behavior is fear that they don't measure up. And because of that fear, they are compelled to try and overwhelm you with all they know or all they have accomplished in life. They don't need our derision, even when we may want to express that. They need our empathy and our prayers that they can see themselves as the whole human beings they are.

How blessed we are that God sends not one of us away—ever. He is always in the wings awaiting our need, whatever it is. As I've expressed myriad times in other meditations, God is our constant companion whether we acknowledge Him or not. He will not leave our side. He will anticipate our every need. All we have to do is surrender to His guidance and life will run smoothly.

God's presence is as certain as our breath—and will always remain so.

10.
Life is sometimes very difficult and painful and we don't feel prepared for it.
—Thelma Elliott

Nearly every day we are faced with something we don't really feel prepared for. That's the natural rhythm of life. And yet, some spiritual paths suggest we are always prepared for everything that comes our way because each experience is naturally evolving from whatever happened before. *There are no accidental experiences*, many would say.

Of course, that doesn't mean we might not be overwhelmed by some experiences anyway, but we can handle them, every one of them, or they wouldn't have arrived on our horizon. Turning to the God of our understanding for support will allow us to walk through whatever pain or difficulty or confusion confronts us. We can count on this with certainty. And that promise makes life less difficult, doesn't it?

We are always in the right place at the right time having the perfect experience, but that doesn't mean we don't need God's help to walk through it.

11.

In order to accept change and the suffering it brings, we need to find meaning in it.
—Mary Norton Gordon

At the core of every change that beckons is timing. Any change that intersects our journey has been specifically invited by us, if not consciously, then at an unconscious level. Change is natural and necessary if we are to make any progress as we navigate life. And we intuitively know this even if we feel unprepared for the change, even if we may find ourselves pained by it and fight it for a time. It's okay to resist the change initially; that's evidence of our human fears. But eventually, we must surrender. Our inner self knows we need the changes that come, every one of them.

The meaning within any change is obvious as soon as we are willing to see how it advances our progress. We must finally recognize this if we are to fully celebrate the life we have been so lovingly allowed to live. Never forget: our life is a partnership with God.

Today, as is true every day, we are in the company of God. We need not fret. All is well.

12.

If I can stop one heart from breaking, I shall not live in vain.
—Emily Dickinson

Do we really have the power to stop someone's heart from breaking? I think not. I don't actually think that's our job. But we do have the power, if we are so inclined, to offer compassion and a soft shoulder to the soul who is hurting as the result of life's oftentimes unexpected circumstances. Although some may believe, as I do, that no circumstance is truly unexpected, that every one of them is part of the natural trajectory of one's life, that doesn't mean we will necessarily remember this when in the throes of a change we had "forgotten" was coming.

Allowing ourselves to be loving and kind through our compassionate desire and willingness to aid a fellow traveler struggling over a lost love, a lost job, or a lost family member is always the right thing to do. However, that's not the same as sheltering them from the pain of the loss. That's not our job. Feeling the loss is part of letting go of that which needed to pass from our lives. Everything has its time, both to be with us and to leave. Let's rejoice in knowing this.

Being willing to release what needs to go is a sign of real progress on this long road we travel. Helping someone hang on to what needs to go helps no one. Nurture freedom instead.

13.

Pain is inevitable: suffering is optional.
—Haruki Murakami

The choice to suffer over the changing currents of our lives is always ours to make. But there is another choice, and that's the primary decision every experience is offering us. We may have multiple opportunities every day to make that decision, in fact. We have all met people who seem to relish suffering; sadly, they may see it as a way to get attention. But suffering is never mandatory. Even in the direst circumstances, we can choose to see the situation as something whose time has come. And that changes one's outlook immediately.

Accepting the fact that painful experiences will befall us all and that it's quite natural for those experiences to be part of the "lesson plan" of our lives is another definition of wisdom. We aren't simply skating through this life. We are here to learn, to grow, and to help others on their way. Pain may well accompany any one of these activities, and our response can be, *"Acceptance is the answer to all situations."* If we make that choice, we will comfortably move forward.

Pain is not the be-all and end-all of our lives. It's natural and it may be frequent, but it need not trouble us at all.

14.
God is the only constant.
—Ruth Casey

God is the only constant we need, I'd say. However, change is a constant too. But these two constants dovetail nicely. God helps us handle all the changes we inevitably experience throughout our lives, if we turn to Him. And that's a big if. Not everyone is a believer. There was a time in my distant past when I wasn't a believer either. What I have come to appreciate, however, is that God always believed in me, even when I didn't believe in Him.

Because God is a constant in our lives, we can discard worry once and for all. We will never face anything that can't be handled with God's help. Never. Now, it's necessary for us to turn to Him willingly, but even if we don't, He waits in the wings and helps out anyway. We will simply never be left adrift. We will be led to the right outcome, whatever the circumstance. There is always a right outcome, and God is always on duty.

Not only is God a constant, He is our comforter in all situations. We need not worry ever again. We are free.

15.

It is a mistake to look too far ahead. Only one link in the chain of destiny can be handled at a time.
— Sir Winston Churchill

Getting ahead of ourselves, not "living where our feet are planted," is perhaps the most common failing we all share. And we need not feel ashamed. It's the heightened anticipation about what might be coming later today, later this week, or even later this year that pulls us away from settling for just being in this moment. The idea of clinging to one moment at a time and living it fully feels foreign to many of us and therefore unattainable. And without a serious commitment to living one moment at a time, it will slip away.

We are so easily caught off guard by thoughts of the future, a future that may well never materialize. It's not necessarily because thoughts about the present aren't of interest or at times even fascinating. But it's so human of us to wonder about what might be coming next. When that's where our attention rests, we miss the activity in this moment completely. And when we do that habitually, we really aren't *living* at all. In all actuality, there is nothing but this specific moment — one specific moment after another. And when we forget to live this way, we forget to live. Period.

Life, moment by moment, is really far simpler to live than one might imagine. We need only make up our minds to give this a try.

16.

The crucial task of old age is balance.
— Florida Scott-Maxwell

I am actually inclined to say that the crucial task of *any* age is balance. And balance is achieved by living a more moderate life. Many love living at the extremes, where excitement reigns. You could have counted me among that group in days of old. However, on the extreme edges is where we tend to create conflict and unrest with others. Perhaps that's what some are seeking. Personally, I want to live more peacefully. I have discovered God is more present to me when I am focused on being peaceful, and that's more interesting now.

To each his own, however; so I say to those who want the thrill of living on the edge, just be careful. Slipping off is easy to do. Additionally, setting that kind of example might well lead someone to follow you who can never find their way back. It's true we aren't responsible for the choices of others. But we are responsible for serving others in a positive way. Being ever mindful of that is a sure sign of choosing the balanced life.

Making the decision upon arising of how we want to live the day makes choosing the actions that will move us in that direction far easier. It's about having a plan, isn't it?

17.
The first duty of love is to listen.
— Paul Tillich

Offering truly rapt attention to those who are traveling this road with us is the primary opportunity we have to express our love. When asked, most of us would probably claim to be good listeners. But that's often not the case. We "hear" the words perhaps, but do we listen between the lines? Do we listen to the heart that's seeking to be heard? Do we hear the nuggets of pain or joy that are embedded in the words?

Just turning toward the speaker isn't a true sign of listening, and we all know we have been guilty of that. Really listening is about allowing our own minds to be empty, for the moment, so that we can fully absorb that which is being uttered. Let's not be ashamed to admit that we are often poor listeners. That's the first step toward becoming committed to developing the *art* of true listening. And I do mean "art." True listening is a far different way of receiving the words of others, and the gift to both speaker and listener is rich indeed.

Truly listening to those who journey with us is the only "assignment" we have today. Let's score high.

18.

You may be one person to the world, but you
may also be the world to one person.
—Audrey Hepburn

We so easily underestimate our value to the people in our lives.
It's helpful to remember that no one sharing our path is there
accidentally. We all needed to encounter each other or we would
not have shown up. That's a powerful realization. That means every
single person you have been engaged by, throughout your life, had
a reason to wander your way. Many of those encounters were of
course dismissed, and the failing is that then we will never know
what gift we failed to receive.

It's not that hard to decide to look at each person with a bit more
interest and respect. We may not know why someone has come our
way, but God knows, and God has planned the meeting. For us to
discount it denies both of us the blessing the scheduled meeting
was intended to bestow. Let's simply assume that we need to
acknowledge everyone who wanders our way, if only for a few brief
minutes. That way we won't cheat them or ourselves.

Let's accept as an absolute truth that we are important to everyone we meet
today, friend or stranger. How much easier all decisions would be.

19.

What the caterpillar calls the end of the
world, the master calls a butterfly.
—Richard Bach

The tapestry of our lives is beautifully woven, and every thread
is necessary to the final design. Each thread is of course symbolic
of an experience, with each one as necessary as the passing of the
caterpillar, who can only become a butterfly when its work is done.
We cannot move to the next phase of our lives either, not until
we have completed the one we are in. And if we then lament the
passage to the next phase, we must remember that no earlier phase
has been unintended or superfluous.

It's a relief to be able to realize that nothing is for naught. We may not like some of the things we go through, but if we are willing to review the myriad experiences we have had already, we will see how perfect each one was in the way it launched us forward into the next perfect experience. Surrendering to the perfection of our lives, even when we stumble and sometimes have to backtrack, is the final way forward to true understanding. We will always be exactly where we need to be for whatever so perfectly calls us next.

Resting in the awareness that we are always exactly where we need to be right now makes living so much easier. Why fight it?

20.
We can trust in the constancy of one thing; time will always move forward.
—Amy E. Dean

Time is elusive. It doesn't stand still, but there are periods in our life when it definitely seems to drag. We all remember how long school days seemed to last when we were kids, and then, in comparison, how short summer vacation seemed. When in the midst of an experience that's joyful, we want time to slow down. And then there are those dreaded experiences. They are the ones that so often feel like they are taking forever to pass.

This awareness should clearly reveal to us that time is always a reflection of our own minds, our own choosing. It's true clocks gently tick the time away, and that any clock is comparable to any other clock in this respect; yet how we respond to those passing moments and hours is directly reflective of our response to the events taking place in that time.

In and of itself, time simply is. We give it all the meaning it will ever have.

Today will afford me the opportunity to appreciate the passage of time and each experience I am given in that time frame. It will help if I embrace each moment as it comes.

21.
There is no healing without forgiveness.
—Helen Casey

The power of forgiveness cannot be overestimated. And we have to be willing to forgive everyone for everything, no matter how insignificant the seeming infraction may have been. When we resist forgiving someone, we are actually holding everyone else hostage too. We may not have realized it, but our unforgiveness of anyone separates us from everyone else. The refusal to forgive imprisons all of us. The entire human community suffers as a result.

There are many who believe that it is ourselves who ultimately need to be forgiven, that what we think others did to us, we actually projected onto them. The oft-forgotten adage that when we point a finger at someone else, three fingers are pointing back at us is the principle at work here.

It boils down to this: forgiveness allows people to rejoin at a spirit level, and that's where the healing of the heart happens.

The main goal of life is helping one another, and this helps all hearts heal. The pathway there is forgiveness. Am I on board with this idea today?

22.
Grace is when we notice the near-misses we survived
instead of the wishes that didn't come true.
—Nancy Hull-Mast

Our lives have been blessed by many near-misses. It's far too easy to overlook them due to our incessant focus on what we hoped would happen, but didn't. As we grow in wisdom, we finally begin to see that grace has played an important role throughout our lives. We often referred to grace as luck, but it is far more than luck. God has intervened in our lives as he is likely to do whenever we stand too close to the edge.

Living on the edge is very seductive. Before entering the rooms of recovery from addictions, I loved living on the edge. I came to see that I'd have slipped over more than once if God had not graced me with His presence. We can all see these times in our past if we sit a spell and review them. Whenever I am feeling at a loss, it's my practice to remember how God's presence has blessed me again and again. The gratitude I feel when I remember this is what shakes me free from depression when it edges up close to me.

God was always there. Our lives were always graced by His presence. Revisiting our past will reveal the multitude of divine visits. Grace has repeatedly been our companion.

------------------------------ 23. ------------------------------

Anger dwells only in the bosom of fools.
—Albert Einstein

Note that Einstein didn't say avoid anger period. He said, *don't dwell on anger.* And we all have experienced the long-term effects of anger that we have hung onto for lengthy periods. The results of holding onto anger are never good for us emotionally, physically, or mentally. And perhaps the worst effect is that our anger interferes with all of our relationships. We aren't free to enjoy any experience or any relationship if we are harboring anger, even when the person we are with isn't the focus of our anger.

Anger eats away at our peace of mind. I think we can safely say that there can be no peace of mind if we are held in the grip of anger. And a peaceful mind is necessary if we want to experience peaceful relationships. Anger is often triggered by an intentional slight or even a sideways comment, but we can choose to step aside from that experience. Understanding that someone else's anger is rooted in the condition of their own mind and not at all in us makes letting it go far easier.

To be peaceful requires that we let the brief moments of anger slip away. We have the capacity to choose who we want to be in every instance. Let's take it.

------ 24. ------

Letting go is an ongoing commitment.

How nice it would be to let go, just once, and then sit back and watch our lives unfolding more peacefully. But that isn't how it works for most of us. In fact, in my eighty-one years, I have never met a person who was able to let go completely on the first attempt. What I generally observe, and it's what I do too, is that one tends to reclaim control in almost the next breath.

We have to practice letting go, almost with a vengeance, and I personally think that's good, perhaps even a path preferable to that of the very few who accomplish it more quickly. The practice is good because with each attempt we are turning to the God of our understanding for assistance, and that's never without benefit.

Letting go accomplishes two key things; it allows the other person to live the life they are choosing to live, and it frees us to live our own lives in unison with God, not the person we are trying to control. This is truly a beneficial choice.

There is no time like this moment to practice letting go of that person who is sitting in the center of your mind. She will be grateful, and so will you.

------ 25. ------

You can't hear your inner voice if your mind is on someone else.

Our minds are far too often busy with thoughts of others—usually thoughts of how to best control them. And all the while our inner voice tries to get our attention to dissuade us from our attempts. But we can't entertain two thoughts at once, and generally our desire to control wins out. The end result, however, is failure after failure. No matter how hard we try or how self-righteous our attempts may be, we simply will never be able to control the uncontrollable. And the inner voice was attempting to help us see this all the while.

Because it comes from God, the inner voice never disappears, but we can drown it out, and we often do. How persistent it is—fortunately, every bit as persistent as our attempts to control the behavior of others. In time, we will give up our attempts to control, and God will still be waiting to give us comfort and the more perfect direction we need. Just knowing that God never leaves our side, no matter how dismissive we have been, is the awareness we need to finally turn and listen to His voice once and for all.

Listening to God is not a hard decision to make. And it is one that promises peace of mind. Today is a great day to choose peace.

26.

Healing opportunities wear coats of many colors.

The opportunities we experience every day to heal our minds and hearts are vast in number. But unless we are accustomed to watching for them, we will often miss them. However, if we could choose to see every encounter as a potential opportunity for healing two hearts, we'd be on the right path. All it takes is the willingness to reach out in a loving way to whomever is standing before us. And every time we practice reaching out in this way, we are changing the discourse of everyone.

It is said that what we do for one, we do for everyone. That is a simple principle to live by. It encourages us to pause before doing or saying anything. If we are showing up in a helpful way, proceed. If we are not prepared to do that, we need to pause again.

The easiest way to wend our way through the day is to ask ourselves in every encounter: are we being truly helpful? If not, make the adjustment that's necessary. Being helpful is the only goal we will ever need.

Every experience today will offer us a chance to heal ourselves and others. Let's not let any chance slip away.

27.

Love cures. It cures those who give it
and cures those who receive it.
— Dr. Karl Menninger

There may not be a more important proponent of the value of love than Dr. Menninger. His statement is uncompromising. Love is the pathway to healing, and no one is ever singularly healed. Healing is collaborative, just as love is collaborative. The very idea that love cures should make us all jump with joy over how very attainable healing even the most emotionally affected people can be with time and willingness.

The Menninger Clinic has made use of this simple antidote to mental illness for all of its years of existence. That's not to say, however, that everyone is healed, or healed quickly. But with love as the conduit to healing, everyone at least has a fighting chance as long as he or she is open to being loved back to health. Of course that's the key. Openness to healing has to be the first step. We must want a different life in order to receive one. This is true for all of us, no matter how mentally stable we may be at the moment.

We need to ask ourselves every day if we are the people we want to be. If the answer is no, the next question is: how might our willingness to love and be loved help us? Let's explore this today.

28.

Our relationships always reflect our state of mind.

There is no wiggle room in this statement. The equation is as follows: when we are peaceful, our relationships are peaceful too. If we are caught in a moment of agitation, this too will show up quickly in how we are behaving in the relationship that currently has our attention. Whomever we are "in here" is exactly who we experience "out there." The good news about this state of affairs is that we can change our minds, and our relationships will change too—in the blink of an eye!

This idea may seem too simple to be true, but test it out. The next time you are feeling stress or agitation, take notice of how you are interacting with the people close at hand. Then take the opportunity to pause and seek to see yourself and the situation differently, and then notice a second time how you are feeling in the midst of the interaction. You will have changed. For certain, you will have changed. Our state of mind does indeed define our relationships in the moment.

Our relationships will be as peaceful as we want them to be. We are in charge of the changes that need to be made.

29.

The most important thing we are doing
right now is thinking nice thoughts.
— Jim and Marie Burns

Jim and Marie are lovely people I had the good fortune to meet
when I was writing a meditation book for the aging population. I'd
venture to say they had very few thoughts that were not nice ones,
and the example they set for others is one we should all emulate.

There is nothing so very difficult about thinking nice thoughts. It's a
decision, but it is one that needs to be followed up by action. Other
than while meditating, we are generally thinking one thought or
another every instant of our life. Deciding to make even some part
of them nice would go a long way toward changing the world we
share with others for the better.

But maybe we need to define more specifically what a nice thought
is. It never causes hurt feelings. It elevates others, always. It's
kind and loving, never demeaning. It invites others in rather than
holding them at bay. It's gentle.

*Making the decision today to cultivate nice thoughts in all our affairs will
allow us to feel the peace we crave. It will also nurture peaceful feelings in
those we encounter as well.*

30.

There are many realities. We should remember
this when we get too caught up in being concerned
about the way the rest of the world lives.
— Natalie Goldberg

It's a common reaction to assume the people around us see the
world as we see it. When we realize they don't, our judgment often
rears its ugly head. Allowing for myriad realities is the pathway to
peace, however, and it encourages us to appreciate that a variety of
perspectives makes for fascinating discussions if we can get beyond
the narrow idea that only our own way of seeing is correct. It's not
accidental when we have crossed paths with someone who sees a

situation from a different perspective. We needed to be offered this new way of seeing, or it would not have shown up.

Being stuck in our own reality curbs our intellectual and emotional growth. How fortunate we are that every day our circumstances introduce us to many other ways of seeing. And with each new awareness comes the opportunity to bask in appreciation and respect for all of the others who travel with us quite intentionally.

That our journeys are perfectly orchestrated is unquestionable. But it's also quite easily forgotten. Let's take careful notice of all the perspectives we are gifted with today.

31.

The process of living is pretty similar for each of us. For every gain, there is a setback. For every success, a failure. For every moment of joy, a time of sadness. For every hope realized, one is dashed.
—Sue Atchley Ebaugh

Growing accustomed to the natural rhythm in our lives, a rhythm that balances out the bad with the good, makes every experience more acceptable and more understandable. It's the differing experiences that enrich us, even when we aren't pleased with how a particular experience might feel while we are in its midst. Growing used to the idea that every experience has its reason for being a part of our life can actually become an exciting way to look at how our lives are unfolding.

Making the decision to celebrate everything that is happening in our lives prepares us for becoming the people we were born to be, the people those who travel beside us need us to be. Remember, there are no unbidden visitors on our path. Everyone has received an invitation from us, oftentimes a forgotten invitation, but one that's been offered nonetheless.

We are on the perfect trajectory for becoming who we have always needed to be. Relax. All is in good order.

JUNE

1.

Love one another but make not a bond of love.
— Kahlil Gibran

Truly loving someone allows for their freedom to love in return. Many mistakenly interpret love as clinging to someone or keeping them beholden to us for their security and ours, but that's not love at all. That's hostage taking; true love must allow the other person to flee if that's their wish.

Love is seldom easy in the early stages because of the freedom to grow and change that each person must allow the other as they come together. Actually, most relationships aren't based on love when they first begin. At the outset, each person is in search of something they think they might get from the other person. And then when he or she fails to "pay up," the relationship falters. That's not love. Love seeks nothing but the best for one another.

Love is gentle. It's kind and nurturing. There's never a guarantee when two people come together that they will be able to love wholeheartedly. Being willing to see the presence of God within one another is perhaps the surest pathway to real love. And if that isn't present, don't try to make it so. All will be well.

Love isn't always the outcome when two people come together. Being willing to truly see what's there in front of us is the best guide to love. It's unmistakable.

2.

The very best and utmost of attainment in this life is
to remain still and let God act and speak in thee.
— Meister Eckhart

To remain still, allowing for the time necessary to hear God's words, is such a gentle, simple suggestion and one that will produce results. In the silence, we will receive the guidance we need, but we have to be willing to listen attentively. The message might not be immediately forthcoming. Our patience may in fact be tested, but the guidance will come when the time is right.

How lucky we are that we have this constant partnership that will never let us down. We may not hear what we want to hear, and we may not get the guidance when we think we deserve it, but we will get exactly what we need and at the right time. There's no doubting this. And how fortunate this makes our journey through life. We may still stumble on occasion, but God never fails to help us back up and start us on our way again.

Listen closely today. The message you have been waiting for is on its way.

3.

It's a long trip to serenity. I better start right now.
—Jill Clark

Serenity is actually as close as our next thought. It need not be a distant longing or merely a faraway goal we have set. It truly is as available to us as our desire for it. We set our minds on serenity and it comes into focus. What is it about serenity that is so appealing? The answer to this perhaps may vary a bit for everyone, but in general, it's quiet. It's a time away from the clutter and chatter of other folks we are so often bombarded by. It's a period of going within to find whatever messages might be waiting for us, messages we have perhaps sought to hear from God.

Serenity can actually be experienced in the midst of humdrum life too. Turning our minds off for a moment or allowing them to be still even when all around them is noise is a choice we can make at those times we simply need to steal away. Serenity always waits there.

Our lives are a reflection of what our minds focus on. If we want serenity, choose to focus on it. The stillness will provide it.

4.

What you praise, you increase.
— Catherine Ponder

This quote reminds me of an experience I had a few decades ago.
I had a boss who was brutal to many of his employees. I got the
wrong end of the stick a few times too. But then I was promoted,
and some of the folks who had reported to him became my staff.
One in particular, a young man who was very often criticized by
the boss, made a major improvement in his work while reporting to
me. My former boss was amazed and asked me how I had turned
the young man around. I praised him, I said. My former boss
was dumbfounded.

Praise is what we all deserve. Taking note of the positive traits of
others and highlighting them with praise is sometimes all that's
necessary to change a person's life. We have all experienced this, in
ourselves or someone we know. Praise is the gift we are all capable
of bestowing on others. It is one very small action that is certain to
produce one very big change in someone traveling next to us.

*Praise is a simple gesture, and it's one that changes two lives: both that of the
one being praised and the one giving it.*

5.

Seldom will we remember next week
what bothers us so much today.

The passage of time allows us to get a clearer picture of the
troubling circumstances we are forced to grow through from one
day to the next. Whatever the circumstance, it came on cue as one
of the lessons we had been prepared for. To choose to embrace
all the experiences we have as the lessons we were born to bear
and then share with others changes us significantly—and most
beneficially. Being able to put any experience in perspective is what
ushers in the peace of mind we all seek.

Commonly, if an experience is particularly harrowing, we feel
certain its effects will be with us for a long time. But on the

contrary, even the most trying of situations becomes understandable in time, and if we are patient we grow in gratitude for them too. With just a bit of willingness, we are able to embrace the wisdom that comes from learning that no experience is without a lesson— one that we need and one our companions need as well.

We can breathe easily today, knowing that whatever experience presents itself, we will soon understand its significance and be grateful for it.

6.

Be kind to everyone, and start with the person standing next to you.
—Mother Teresa

There is no simpler suggestion for conveying peace and goodwill than these few words spoken by Mother Teresa. Making the decision to be kind, with no exceptions, is the solution to all that ails this world. Perhaps this sounds too simplistic. But if this suggestion were taken by our leaders throughout the world as words to live by and accepted as well by members of our communities and family units, everything would change—absolutely everything.

Current conditions in the world are so often in the hands of bullies and master manipulators who consider kindness a weakness. It's quite likely that the change I'm favoring begins from the bottom up. And that is something each one of us has control over. We can begin each day by making a promise to ourselves that we will pause before saying anything, just to monitor ourselves. If what we are on the verge of saying isn't kind, we still have a chance to be our better selves in that moment. And the experience will then be one we can feel proud of as the day progresses.

We have great power to change the tenor of every encounter we have today. Let's embrace the words of Mother Teresa and make this a kinder world, one person at a time.

7.

You start preparing at thirty for the person you will be at eighty.
— Janice Clark

Looking at our lives from this perspective encourages us to embrace
the importance of every event that visits us on our journey. Each
one of them is helping us develop into being the person meant to
fulfill a perfect role in the lives of all the people who journey with
us. As I've said myriad times throughout these pages, no encounter
we have is unintentional. Each party to the experience will take
away exactly what he or she needs to move forward on her path.

Life is laid out so perfectly, isn't it? Even when we feel certain that
things are amiss, they aren't. We simply haven't gotten on board
with the evolution of the experience. The fact we each must finally
accept is that we are not in charge of the rhythm of the events in
our lives. We are students before we are teachers. All is happening
in perfect order; that is the certainty. Each experience is grooming
us for who we need to be, and that makes living each one of them so
much more acceptable.

Looking forward from today, knowing that whatever comes is preparing us for
our many tomorrows, makes each experience that much more valuable.

8.

All problems work out, though not always
the way you want them to.
— James Casey

Simple philosophies are so often the kindest. For sure they are the
easiest to grasp and to live by. Making the decision to embrace the
idea that all problems do ultimately work out for the best opens the
door to far easier navigation through life.

Embracing the idea that there is a Higher Power in charge of how
the experiences of our lives are playing out and how they neatly fit
together offers us the opportunity to sit back, breathe more easily,
and simply agree to the pattern that our life is weaving. We don't
need to question our experiences as they present themselves. They

are showing up at their perfect time for our perfect growth and well-being. Making the decision to accept this idea will make every moment so much easier to embrace.

God is saying, "Give up the control. I have all of this handled." Our lives are only made complicated because we fight the gift God is offering us.

9.
God knows no distance.
— Charleszetta Waddles

These four simple words remind me of something my mother-in-law told me many decades ago when I was struggling to know God: "If you feel far from God, it's not because He moved." Getting a handle on the idea that God is within, always as close as our next breath, isn't all that easy when one is feeling bereft and disconnected. We have all been there, probably multiple times.

But the truth of our lives is that God didn't move. God never moves away from us. Our own fear blocks our awareness of His presence, but His presence is never gone. For some of us, it becomes necessary to practice believing in the presence of God. Begin by just talking to God as though he's a friend you are having a secret visit with. The more one normalizes these visits, the more apparent it becomes that God really is present, here and now.

Let's not make God a stranger today. He is as present as we are, and He always will be.

10.
We learn from every experience, in retrospect,
that everything has turned out perfectly.
— Robbie Dircks

This principle explains so definitively how our lives are unfolding. It takes the fretting out of each day if we embrace it as the truth of our lives. And all we really have to do is review our past to check how accurate this idea is. All of those times we were so certain some terrible calamity was about to strike, we were nudged to turn a corner or open a new door. At the time, we may not have gathered what role God was playing, but a perfect outcome was being orchestrated—again and again.

Our lives are full of perfect outcomes. Nothing that has happened during our journey has been without purpose. That's not to imply every experience has been pleasant. Indeed not. But whatever the experience was, it was necessary to what was planned next for us. If we could only remember this in our moments of doubt. We have not been abandoned to the throes of any experience without a guide who can make sense of it. That's a promise.

Let's remember today that in the end, all is well. We will always be led in the right direction to play our part in each perfect outcome.

11.
Sharing secrets requires trust.
Accepting secrets requires an open heart.
—Kathleen Tierney Andrus

Being able to trust a friend with something deep and personal about ourselves is the doorway to meaningful emotional growth for both people. The friends who do travel with us are the natural recipients of our innermost secrets. But we still may not initially be willing to open ourselves fully by revealing what we have kept hidden away. It's good to consider that the frequent presence of friends in our lives just may be an indication that God has sent them our way for the very purpose of being our trusted listeners.

And then when friends share their secrets with us in turn, it touches us deeply. Because of our own experiences, we realize the depth of their trust in us, which blesses us and makes us feel connected and whole. The sharing of secrets is a gift we all are given the opportunity to both give and receive. It might actually be considered the glue that solidifies a real friendship. Knowing this is a role we are invited to play with a friend changes us in a good way.

Being available to a friend who wants to share something personal today just might be our greatest opportunity for growth. It surely is a great gift for both parties, one that leads to peace of mind.

12.

We are empowered to have exactly the kind of day we want to have every day.

How fortunate that we are given this gift for living each day. Having a life that's at the whim of someone else's behavior means not really having our own life at all. While it's true that we are continuously interacting with others and that those interactions do play at least a momentary role in who we become, that's not the same as being at the mercy of those others. We get to pick and choose the interactions we want to nourish, and that makes all the difference.

Learning to live in the company of others, yet not beholden to them for our personal growth and well-being, is the gateway to having the peace of mind we all deserve, no matter what stage of life we are in. Being empowered to experience only peace may seem beyond what any of us can expect; however, that's not the case. We simply have to be determined and make the choice to let all else pass us by. Making that choice on a regular basis will define us as we want to be defined.

We can choose to experience a peaceful journey every day. Today is a great day to give this a try.

13.

There is good in every experience. We simply must be willing to see it.

No adversity can hold us back for long if we look to our Higher Power for guidance and direction. Any experience that feels uncertain just hasn't yet been turned over to the God of our understanding. All our experiences will weave themselves together for our good.

We are living a charmed life. We may not always know that everything is perfect as is and that our experiences are moving us toward the peaceful lives we all deserve and desire; but that is, in fact, the promise of this journey. Nothing happens that isn't meant for our good when it shows up in our lives — nothing at all.

We are always being cared for in a most perfect way. Our pathway to peace is guaranteed.

14.

The deepest need of man is the need to overcome his separateness, to leave the prison of his aloneness.
—Erich Fromm

We all know what it feels like to enter a gathering of people and feel distant, separate, or alone even though we are part of a crowd. It's a deadly feeling, yet our sense of aloneness is a false interpretation. We are never alone. God is always as close as our next breath. In fact, we would have no breath without His presence. We feel separate because we are listening to the ego, which is the home of fear. The good news is that we can quit listening to the ego right now.

We all need one another. It's through our connections to each other that we are introduced to the lessons we were born to learn and to teach. Life is a classroom, and we are all students and teachers, first one and then the other. The give-and-take is what creates the rhythm of our lives. And it's in the give-and-take that we come to appreciate peace, and experiencing peace is our ultimate life lesson.

We are here to experience peace and help one another experience it too. Today will be full of opportunities.

15.

We all live with the objective of being happy; our lives are all different and yet the same.
—Anne Frank

Abraham Lincoln is supposed to have said: *We are as happy as we make up our minds to be.* Whether or not he actually said that is not so very important; what is important is the truth of the statement. We indeed are as happy as we decide to be. And that's the will of God. What makes us all so very interesting on this journey we share is the myriad ways we find to discover that happiness. Just as Anne Frank said, we are all different and yet quite the same.

For many, happiness is a byproduct of doing something nice for someone else. Bringing joy into the lives of others makes joy contagious; the giver as well as the receiver both get the payoff. The simplest action may trigger joy in someone else. Even a smile in the direction of a stranger can initiate joy, a joy that can in fact change someone's life. Great things are not required from any one of us to trigger joy in ourselves or others. Simple acts offered lovingly can do the trick.

Let's make today one to remember. Let's keep track of all the times and ways we try to inspire joy in someone else.

16.
The luxury of doing good surpasses every other personal enjoyment.
—John Gay

There is no mystery in the decision to do good; it is a clear and simple choice. And there is no way to be confused as far as what doing good means. All we have to do is ask ourselves one simple question: "Is what I am about to do kind?" If it fails that test, it's a choice that can easily be remade.

Being kind never fails to feel good to the one receiving the kindness. But it also heightens the joy for the person choosing to be kind. How easy life can be when we allow the choice to do good, to be kind, to be helpful to define us.

It's true many activities may make us feel good; for instance, a hot shower, a great home-cooked meal, a massage, or even a yoga class. But the simplicity of simply doing a good and kind act for someone else is hard to beat.

Doing good for others does us so much good as well. And it's a sure way to transform one's life into the peaceful journey we all desire.

17.

Life is perfect just the way it is and just the way it is not.
— Peggy Bassett

Life is perfect. Period. No hedging at all. No stumble on the path is superfluous. No missed opportunity is actually missed at all. Whatever has seemingly passed us by wasn't meant for us after all. What we are meant to experience will definitely not pass us by. And even if we should miss it, it will return. Our lessons are wearing our names.

Adjusting our minds to the idea that everything is always perfect as it is allows us to rest easily throughout the day. We can move through every hour knowing that whatever we need to experience will not escape our notice. With that awareness in mind, we may choose to let an experience ride for now, and that's okay. The peace that comes with looking at our lives from this perspective is nearly beyond description.

Just waking up to the awareness that life really is exactly as it should be gives us freedom to live without worry. This day is another one of God's good gifts.

18.

Man needs difficulties; they are necessary for health.
— Carl Jung

How can it be that difficulties are good for us? What we are learning, again and again, is that the difficult times push us to reach for the outstretched hand of God, which is always extended in our direction. Many of us have not noticed this, in some cases for years, but His hand was always there. It will always be there. God's hand completes the sacred circle that encompasses all of us. Our emotional health is directly tied to our connection to the God of our understanding, and He never leaves our side. We don't even have to notice Him. He will not leave, nor will He quit working on our behalf—ever.

The simple truth is that we are each eventually destined to become aware of God. Our difficulties are invitations to seek His help. God is aware of us and our needs and will be available to fulfill them. There is simply no more certain avenue to well-being than seeking His assistance. We don't really need life's difficulties to push us to seek God, but for some of us, they serve as a launching pad.

Just knowing we need not be troubled by difficulties, that they are what launch us toward God, takes the dread away from them. We are in good hands, always.

19.
The will of God is peace.
—Ernest Holmes

Could any statement be more straightforward? Yet there was a time in my life when trying to discern what God's will was for me drove me crazy. Was it moving to another city? Perhaps taking a different job or ending a troubling relationship? I didn't know how to approach God, so of course, I didn't know how to listen to Him either. Then a friend suggested to me that God's will was far less complicated than I was making it. Coming to believe, as I have, that God's will is quite simply for me to be at peace is doable. But how do we attain peace when we are in the throes of uncertainty? That's the issue.

Choosing peace in the midst of the storm has always been an option. However, it may not come naturally at first. We become very accustomed to reacting in the same old way to everything that happens, and if that reaction is to be anxious, angry, or fearful, it's not easy to suddenly start making another choice. But we can. The pathway to the new response is to pause, think about what we want to feel and do, and then follow through. Choosing peace over and over will in time make it our default position.

Peace is the choice open to us. It's God's will that we make this choice. Today will be as peaceful as we have the will to make it.

20.

**The world is too dangerous for anything but
truth and too small for anything but love.
— William Sloan Coffin**

Striving to tell the truth in a loving way sounds like the perfect way
to journey through life. The guesswork is resolved, once and for all.
Just move gently forward with truth on your lips and love in your
heart, and you will not only be fulfilling the will of God, but the
hope of every person you encounter along the way as well.

We commonly fret about what to do or say in various instances.
Now we know there is only one choice to make: the truth,
expressed lovingly. Being an example of this to everyone
everywhere is the kindest of all ways to navigate through life. How
lucky we are to have this opportunity to choose our path and be
guides along the way for others on the path.

*Who we meet today isn't accidental. Each person is giving us the opportunity
to serve them in the very best way.*

21.

Not all relationships that are right for us are peaceful.

How commonly we assume that when a relationship hits a snag, it's
time to move on. And in some cases, that may be true. But it's often
true that the snags may be a part of the lessons we are here to learn.
Carolyn Myss, the spiritual intuitive who wrote *Sacred Contracts*, said
we meet other souls before arriving here and we agree to experience
certain lessons together. I have come to cherish her perspective. It has
helped me understand so many of the relationships, both good and
bad, that I've had over my eighty-one years. I can trust that each one
of them was necessary for both parties involved.

Additionally, believing this has prepared me to be available for all
the lessons headed my way in the future. As I've said before, no
experience has been unimportant to my growth. Who I am today
(and who you are too) is a composite of all that has happened so far.

We need not dread what may be right around the corner. We have already said yes to it.

We need feel no angst about what lies before us today. Whatever it is, its arrival is on time, and the perfect teacher will accompany it too.

22.

With each new day, I put away the past and discover the new beginnings I have been given.
—Angela L. Wozniak

Being attuned to the day before us guarantees that we will encounter the experiences that have been specifically prepared for us. No fretting is ever necessary. We are in good hands, and we will not be facing any situation without the proper guidance that we need. Making the decision to embrace this understanding of how our lives are unfolding truly does give us peace of mind. For many of us on this path, that has become our ultimate goal.

Looking over our past, even the short view of our past, reminds us of how perfectly our experiences have dovetailed, moving us to the next big growth spurt planned and waiting for us. Every point in our past, every intersection with another person on our path, was by design, never by happenstance. And all of our tomorrows will mimic all of our yesterdays. We can peacefully relax, one day at a time.

Something perfect has been planned for us today. We can count on this and move forward peacefully.

23.

Relationships can always be seen differently.

As I have hinted in other meditations, not every relationship goes smoothly. Sometimes that may mean we need to exit the relationship, at least for a time, but more often choosing to see the relationship differently can help us discern its value for who we are becoming on our journey. The fact of the matter in all instances is that the relationships that attract our attention are there by design. However, it is certainly okay if you are not up to the task of handling a particular relationship. All relationships that are specific to who God is calling us to be will revisit us at another time.

What great relief that offers us. We will receive what we need to receive. Our lives are in divine order. Our experiences are specifically designed for us, and the folks who share them with us need them too. As so many great spiritual thinkers profess, what needs to happen will occur. And we are always in the right place at the right time. We can simply rest and accept the truth of this. All will be well.

We can breathe deeply today trusting fully that all is well. What visits us today will be on our perfect agenda, the one set by God.

24.
God is always present. Never fear.

Trusting that there is a power greater than ourselves in charge of the many outcomes planned for us is key to having any expectation of peace. And that's a pretty good plan for peaceful living one day at a time, a peace which we are always promised if we wait for guidance. It is ever present, but we must be open to it. God is always as close as our next breath. He is our next breath, in fact. Our lives are guaranteed to be peaceful if we keep that awareness uppermost in them.

Few are in constant contact with that "Someone" who is always there. We could be, of course. But we allow the ego, which tries so hard to control our thinking and our actions, to hold sway over so many of our thoughts. The ego's primary job is to keep us agitated and unsure of ourselves. It's not easy to ignore —the ego speaks loudly and pretty constantly in our minds. It takes willingness, coupled with consistent practice, to ignore it, choosing instead to let the God of our understanding help us make the right choices. We can do it if we are persistent.

God is here, now. And He is shaping the events that will visit us today. Each one of them is happening at the perfect time. We can relax, knowing He is in charge.

25.

We all have a purpose in this life, and each day is a step in the journey toward achieving that purpose.
—Kathy McGraw

How sweet it is to be reminded that each one of us does have a purpose in this life. It means that every day we have a task that is ours alone to complete. Early on in my journey, I constantly fretted about what my particular purpose was. I didn't feel like I knew it, and I didn't know how to discern it. Then a friend advised that I was worrying too much about the specifics. He also suggested that making the decision to do no harm was an easily accessible purpose and would fit quite snugly into whatever God expected from me.

Initially, I still felt my purpose had to be more complicated than that. And our purpose does generally mature into something more specific. But beginning with the decision to do no harm means we are on God's trajectory, and He will guide us to the more specific plan He has for us. Ultimately, I discovered that my purpose was to be a writer. It has brought me great peace of mind and near constant contact with my Higher Power, from whom the words flow. Whatever brings us joy is closely tied to our purpose—always.

We are each necessary to the fuller picture of who God is. In fact, we are explicitly necessary to His wholeness; this assures us that we do have a purpose. Listen and you will hear it today.

26.

Every situation can bring us closer to God.

The great news in our lives is that the opportunities to grow closer to God are constant. We need not seek God out. He is present everywhere because He is present within us, and His willingness to guide us never wavers. We may forget how close He is and end up drawing problems to us that we really don't need, but God in essence says, "I will wait until you are ready for Me." And He does.

We really can live problem free. We truly can live as peacefully as we make up our minds to. We really can walk through each day quietly, with full hearts and minds that are focused on the Presence that never leaves. How lucky we are—each and every one of us.

Today invites my attention to be on God for the guidance I will need. He will wait until I am fully ready to seek His guiding hand.

27.
Difficulties push us to reach for the hand of God, and we will soon know that all is well.

It seems counterintuitive to think we need difficulties in our lives, particularly for our health, but they do stretch us to go beyond who we are in the moment. They push us to think in new ways. They encourage us to seek the guidance of others and if that's not forthcoming, to go directly to our Higher Power who will always offer us good orderly direction. In other words, difficulties are necessary if we are to become all that we are meant to be on this journey.

Being glad for difficulties may feel counterintuitive when we greet each new day. We may want to pull the covers over our heads and simply wait for the day to pass. But deciding instead to consider, even for a moment, that God is comfortably wrapped within every difficulty allows us to see these challenges in a wholly fresh way. We will not face any one of them alone. And each one of them is part of our destiny. We may not believe this now, but it's true. Our destiny is perfect and every difficulty we face is perfect for who we are becoming as spiritually and emotionally healthy individuals.

What comes our way has not come haphazardly. To remember this makes all the difference in how we see this day before us.

28.

There can be no defense like elaborate courtesy.
— E. V. Lucas

Courtesy can disarm people, particularly if they aren't expecting it. We have all had occasion to be in the presence of a bully, either as an observer or, worse luck, as the victim. It's never easy to be present in that situation. But responding to the bully courteously rather than in kind can change the tenor of the experience. It may not change him, but it does give us a sense of personal power. Not being at the mercy of a bully is a choice we can make.

Walking away when someone is attempting to lord his or her power over us is a reasonable response. Not engaging with the perpetrator is a safe choice to make. We can choose peace in any situation. Even when our counterpart is trying to engage us in an argument or worse, we can simply say, "Let's reconsider this later," and then walk away. Making the choice over and over to be kind rather than join in a fracas that will lead to heightened tension is extremely wise.

Choosing not to defend ourselves but rather to be a seeker of peace has the capacity to change every experience we may wander into today.

29.

The most important thing I've learned in life is to
love others and accept their love in return.
— Jim Burns

Though it is not always easy to love others unconditionally, doing so makes the journey through this life much less complicated. We can perhaps always find a reason to resist loving any person who doesn't agree with us on issues that are dear to us. We can also resist loving someone for his or her treatment of people we think are deserving of kindness and acceptance. But if we allow ourselves to say no to love in every instance that we feel doesn't meet our standard of what's right, we will find ourselves loving very few people.

Perhaps we'd be better off to decide to love everyone, as we are loved by God. Not only does loving everyone simplify our lives, it guarantees that we will feel better as we journey through life. Allowing ourselves to accept and love others as they are, rather than how we'd prefer they be, is a timesaver. More than that, it encourages a peaceful rhythm that ultimately comforts everyone.

Today will offer us many opportunities to love others regardless of who they are and what they say. That's loving them as God loves us.

30.

The outer world mirrors our inner thoughts in every instance.

Our projections become our perceptions. When we fully absorb the meaning of this, we can see how important it is to monitor what our minds dwell on. Where the mind goes, so goes our attitude, our awareness, and our peace of mind. How easily we let the mind slip into negative places, taking no responsibility for its descent into the rabbit hole of darkness. But just as easily as our focus can slip into a hole, we can shift it and decide once again to hold our thoughts on a higher plane. And when we do, the world we see will reflect the light, the joy, and the peace that emanates from us.

There is really nothing mysterious about this idea once we understand how the mind works. What we see is always what we have chosen to see, regardless of our resistance to this idea. The solution to the profusion of negative outer pictures is to reel the mind back in as quickly as we see it slipping into the darkness. We are in charge, after all. The mind goes only where we allow it to. The work for us is to decide on the outer picture we want and then create it.

This day will look the way we want it to look. Our power to create what we choose to see and experience is awesome.

JULY

1.

God has plans which mortals don't understand.
—Ellease Southerland

We must grow accustomed to the idea that much that is happening in the world around us, as well as in the lives of family members and friends, is beyond our understanding. To embrace this as normal is hard, but God does have the perfect plan for each one of us. Even when what we see on the horizon looks dark or foreboding, we are assured that with God's help we will grow from each experience. And even more, each experience has come at the perfect time and in the perfect way.

Do we really need to understand the ways of God? I think not. Of course, the ego begs to differ. It resists allowing God to be in control; however, no matter how loud it howls, God will win out. To Him, it's not a battle at all. He is simply moving us from point A to point B in order to arrive at point C at the appointed time. We don't need to understand the journey at all. We just need to breathe easily and say amen.

Life is as easy or as hard as we make it. When we decide to let God be the director, the path is smooth.

2.

The only certainty is that nothing is certain.
—Pliny the Elder

These words were written in approximately 78 AD. Times were uncertain, as is still the case. But what was true then and remains true today is that God is always certain and is available to our needs, whatever they may be. But we have to willingly turn to God for the guidance that proclaims certainty and promises well-being. It will be forthcoming.

How lucky we are to have the constant companionship of One who loves us so completely and so unconditionally. Because of that love, anything that feels uncertain to us will be smoothly handled if we allow God to play His part. The only uncertainty that actually exists is what we are trying to control—what we attempt to master with our own excessive efforts at management. We are not needed as managers in this experience of life. Our more proper role is to trust God to lead us where we need to go, to trust Him to smooth the troubled waters, and to listen to His calming words of *All is well.*

Everything that should happen today, will. God is in charge. Let's not forget that.

3.

**The trouble is not that we are never happy;
it is that happiness is so episodical.
—Ruth Benedict**

Happiness can always be our choice, which of course can make it a constant if we are so inclined. That very few of us are inclined to choose happiness in every instance is a conundrum. Some would say that's the power of the ego at work; it really wants to be in charge of every decision we make, and it's not in the ego's best interests to see us happy. Happy people don't choose to create conflicts, and conflicts are the sum and substance of what drives the ego. Therefore, it pushes us to make choices that don't result in our happiness. The insanity of this is obvious to the thoughtful person.

The good news is that we can always make another choice when we see that the decision to be happy is as easily made as one to create conflict, and it's far less stressful too. Choosing the happy pathway means making a more peaceful journey through life. Perhaps maturity makes peace more attractive, although it may simply be that the experience of peace is what makes one inclined to move more frequently in that direction.

Happiness is as available as our decision to choose it. And it will lead us to places we want to return to, again and again.

4.
If a thought is troubling you, choose another one.

What a simple idea. No one is in charge of what we are thinking but ourselves, and our thoughts emanate either from the ego or from the God of our understanding. When the ego is wielding control over our thoughts, we can be pretty certain they will be self-serving at best, and bordering on anger leading to conflict at worst. The problem that troubles so many of us is that we have grown accustomed to letting the ego rule our lives. And because of that, we are far too often stuck in a scenario that can't possibly bring us peace of mind.

Perhaps not everyone is as hungry for peace of mind as I have turned out to be. Sometimes I think it's age that has changed my perspective. At other times, I'm pretty convinced it's because I have simply grown more fond of the quieter life, a way of life that allows me to move through the day free from stress and from a noisy, chattering mind. We all get to choose the journey we are making, and if the more peaceful one appeals to you, assert your prerogative and let those negative thoughts slip away. The choice is solely yours.

Today is ripe with opportunities for peaceful experiences. Our thinking will reflect the choice we make; thus, our lives will as well.

5.
Do not compare yourself with others. Make your own beautiful footprints in the snow.
—Barbara Kimball

How commonly we tend to compare ourselves with friends and even strangers as a matter of practice. The incessant need most of us have to "measure up" is a long-standing trait, owing perhaps to our families of origin, where parents often suggested we should mimic the performance of a sibling in an effort to spur us on. For many of us, this set a pattern that has been hard to break. Becoming aware, and then proud, of the idea that each one of us has unique qualities may not surface until later in life. But now we know, and now we can celebrate the truth of who we are.

There is no one exactly like any one of us. Hallelujah! That's the perfect order of things. In this divine dance which claims all of us as participants, no one has the same steps as you—or me. The beauty of this truth is deserving of celebration. Each one of us is necessary to make the dance complete, and no two roles in the dance are identical. We all fill the stage with beauty and precision at exactly the right time and in the right way. The Choreographer has made it so.

Moving through this day, knowing that it's precisely as it has been choreographed to be, invites a sigh of relief. The dance will go on.

6.

**<div align="center">Love is an act of endless forgiveness,
a tender look which becomes a habit.
—Peter Ustinov</div>**

To choose to live in the bosom of constant forgiveness changes every moment of our lives. It's not that every experience cries out for forgiveness, but each of them does become more rewarding when we fully accept the experience as the perfect lead-in to the next step of our journey. As I've said many times, on this day, we will have an opportunity to experience what's next in our own particular trajectory of encounters. Not a single one of them is unnecessary to the journey we are here to make. However, if we want to slip by a particular experience, that's our call. It will revisit us at another time. It has to revisit us; it is necessary for the full and complete picture of our life to unfold.

It brings us comfort to look with loving eyes on every situation, as well as on all those who are part of it. Knowing this helps us to choose to look with tenderness every time. So little is asked of us as we make our journey from birth to the next experience. Lovingkindness is the easiest route to take.

Today will be rich with experiences wearing our names. Greeting each of them lovingly blesses everyone, not least ourself.

7.

Changing one thing at a time is quite enough.

We have all been obsessed at times with the need to make changes in our lives, believing that not changing is the barrier that's keeping us from experiencing peace of mind. While it's quite true that we may need to make a significant change in how we are navigating life if we want to be at peace, too many of us think we have to change ourselves completely. The truth is that making just one change at a time is far better. Committing ourselves to too many changes at one time doesn't allow us to discern which one of them is key to realizing the peace we seek.

Going slow and being more methodical about the changes we ultimately want to make is, in and of itself, a far more peaceful way to move ourselves forward. Doing too much of anything is overload, even when what we are doing is for the right reasons. Being selective and intentional are far more fruitful ways to proceed.

Changing ourselves for the better will perhaps be an option we are considering today. The decision to move forward should be made only after careful consideration.

8.

For this is wisdom: to live, to take what
fate, or the Gods, may give.
—Laurence Hope

Accepting the experiences that come to us as the absolute gifts of God eases our journey because it alleviates the guesswork in our search for specific meaning. God is in the hand of everything that pays us a visit. This realization allows us to breathe more easily within whatever experience has chosen us as its recipient. In other words, we can celebrate everything as the perfect offering from God for the next leg of our journey.

Making the decision to believe that God is, in fact, giving us each experience that comes our way makes our acceptance of it so much easier. He has chosen it for us because of our need to learn what it can teach us. Obviously, we won't have to handle whatever it is alone; God accompanies the experience. God and the experience are One just as God is One with us. The order of everything in our life is divine, and believing this allows for true peace of mind.

We can rest today knowing that we have always been in good hands. God has never abandoned us to any experience that wasn't perfect for our well-being. In fact, He walked us through each one as it came.

9.

To behave with dignity is nothing less than to allow others freely to be themselves.
— Sol Chaneles

Being willing to let others be whoever they are choosing to be isn't always easy. The inclination to want to change others, generally in order to satisfy one's own need for security, is an all-too-common response to people traveling the path with us. It takes great willingness to allow them to be themselves and to make whatever choices please them, particularly when we feel certain those choices are wrong. Real dignity comes from the willingness to let everyone, ourselves included, conduct themselves in accord with the dictates of their own conscience.

Everyone deserves the freedom to make whatever choices fit into the picture they are creating of themselves. And we must all respect, even celebrate, that no two such pictures are alike and that each picture is perfect in its composition.

Having the opportunity to celebrate the choices someone else is making today is why we are present with them on the path. Our presence is never accidental.

10.

Nobody told me how hard and lonely change is.
— Joan Gilbertson

Most of us feel rankled by the mere mention of change. Even if we don't love our current circumstances, the prospect of changing them is seldom very appealing. Change implies the unknown, and we shudder at how the unknown might present itself. Living with what is known, unpleasant though it may be, seems far less risky to most of us.

But change is good. It's a sign that we are ready for the next phase of our development, even though we may not realize it. We seldom remember that God is actually in charge of the changes that are occurring in our lives. Their timeline is His, not ours. Being willing to accept this as the natural rhythm of our lives allows us to be far more flexible and to trust that whatever presents itself has absolutely not come unexpectedly. We may not have known it was on the way, but the spiritual forces at work in our lives knew it. We can relax.

There is truly not a single thing we need to worry about. God is always in charge of things, whether they change or remain the same.

11.

We need others physically, emotionally, intellectually; we need them if we are to know anything, even ourselves.
—C. S. Lewis

There may be a time in one's life when you feel you don't need anyone at all, or at least don't want to need anyone. The idea of being truly independent may appeal to us during certain phases of our life. However, the underlying need for others never leaves us. Without our fellow travelers around us, we'd simply not be introduced to all the lessons we were born to experience, lessons that are in turn shared with others at the perfect time in their development.

As has been stipulated before, nothing happens accidentally. Our journeys are quite intentional; our meetings with others are specific to a timeline that serves them as it serves us; we have been called to be where we are. Let's not only remember this but celebrate it. Our path has been carefully laid out for us. Our part is to follow it and lovingly greet all those we meet along the way. That's why they have shown up.

Life is really pretty simple. Our egos want to complicate it, but God says no. Just allow those you meet to know that they matter.

---------- 12. ----------

It is the very pursuit of happiness that thwarts happiness.
—Viktor E. Frankl

How often we are certain that some one thing will make us happy—
so we go after it, only to discover that getting it doesn't measure
up to our anticipation around the acquisition or achievement.
The lesson here is that seeking outside of ourselves for anything
isn't where real joy is ever found. God is our source of joy and
happiness, and God is within. When we go within and listen to the
guidance that's been waiting for us all along, we discover we need
do nothing to claim it. It is simply ours, and it is most easily found
in the midst of bringing joy to someone else.

Viktor Frankl was an amazing human being. He survived the
concentration camps and can surely serve as an exemplar for us of
the gift that lies in making love of humanity our commitment. And
within that commitment, we will know happiness. That which we
seek was there with us all the time.

Appreciate today for the gift of happiness it will offer unbidden. Then share it
with others. What we give away we get to keep.

---------- 13. ----------

No thought of fear can enter a mind while it thinks of God.

We cannot hold two thoughts at the same time. How truly fortunate
that is. It's the easy pathway to peace of mind, because if we are
harboring a thought that is unkind toward someone else or a fearful
thought about a situation in our own lives, all we have to do is let
it pass and think instead of God. Peace will then fill our minds and
comfort us.

So much about our lives would feel less stressful if we remembered
this easy access to peace of mind. In the midst of any inner storm,
quietly repeating "God" will alleviate the turmoil in that very
moment. Moving through each day with peace as well as joy in our
hearts is as available to us as we desire. But it's our call. It's our
decision, always, to call out to God. He is always present.

Nothing could be easier today than turning our minds over to God, even momentarily. Then take notice of how free from turmoil we feel. The only thought we will ever need if we want peace of mind is the thought of God.

14.
Listening to a caring friend is one of the ways we can hear God's message.

We no doubt have an opportunity every day to listen to a caring friend. It is such a gift to be reminded that in each conversation, God is present and sharing something we need to know. What this implies is that we are never far from God's message, but we seldom appreciate how really close at hand it is. He wants to reach us to help us navigate the journey to which we are called.

It's our job each day to pay close attention to every word a friend is sharing. Each word is full of meaning because God is always prompting the messenger. Looking at our lives and God's presence in them from this perspective makes the journey feel so much smoother and safer. No visitor on our path comes alone; she is always accompanied by God.

Let's turn our attention to the voices that are present on our journey today. They are coming straight from God.

15.
We must not ignore the small daily differences we can make, which, over time, add up to big differences that we often cannot foresee.
—Marian Wright Edelman

Every day we have multiple opportunities to offer tiny kindnesses to the men and women we encounter on our daily journeys. We most often assume they have wandered onto our path accidentally, but nothing could be further from the truth. They came because it was on their agenda to be here, just as it was on ours. As I've said many times, we will meet no accidental visitors today. And being reminded of that can certainly alleviate any fear we may conjure up about what or who the day will bring.

Nothing will happen today that shouldn't; however, we can smooth any rough patch that might be triggered by being a gentle participant or even just a gentle onlooker. A gentle presence is the kind of small difference that will never be overlooked by those who are seeking acceptance and compassion. Our part in the grand scheme of things is both huge and yet tiny. But never question the fact that we do have a part.

It's a particularly thrilling realization that we are on a mission today. And our assignment, though perhaps tiny, is absolutely necessary to the rhythm of the universe.

16.
Everything passes, and as I flow with this river of highs and lows, I become calm.
— Ruthie Albert

The simple reminder that everything passes allows us to breathe more deeply. Even though experience has shown us that nothing lasts forever — neither the bad nor the good — while in the midst of something harrowing, it's often hard to relax and wait for it to pass. Reflection confirms that it will pass, but we must be willing to reflect. There are also those times, infrequent though they may be, when we are so trapped by the fear of the instance itself that we can't even be open to reflection.

That's when remembering that we do have a Higher Power who is willing to help us over every stumbling block makes life so much more peaceful. And the really fortunate fact is that even when we fail to remember God, He has not forgotten us and is pulling a few strings even though we haven't requested His specific help. He is always on duty. That's the miracle of our lives. We don't even have to request His help for it to be there. It can't be any other way.

We are assured today that nothing will trouble us for long. We can be certain of upsets. That's the rhythm of life, but we can be even more certain of God's help.

17.

The feeling remains that God is on the journey too.
— St. Teresa of Avila

What idea could be simpler or more true? Wherever we are, God is. Period. And if that idea doesn't give you peace of mind, it's doubtful that anything will. We really need not be concerned about our journey today, or any day. The specifics have already been selected for us, and we do not journey alone. It's a pretty simple picture. And every aspect of our experiences fits quite comfortably into the overall picture that our lives have been weaving so far. There isn't any mystery about how it's going to go; it's just that we aren't privy to the mystery ahead of time.

Personally, I think being apprised of this kind of evolution in our lives makes them all the more exciting. Where we will go is known, just not to us in the moment. Who we will journey with is known as well. The full picture will become known to us in the right way and at the right time. Our part is to trust that since God is always journeying with us, all is *always* well.

Today will be perfect however it transpires.

18.

Life is so much easier if you ride the
horse in the direction it's going.
— Werner Erhard

How often do we bang our heads against the wall trying to change an unyielding situation or a person who is unchangeable, at least in that moment? This may well be all too common for many of us. However, we can make another choice. We can allow others to be who they choose to be, and we can allow situations to unfold in a more natural way. Making these choices for ourselves promises much deserved relief along with serenity.

We will never get someone else to do something against their will, regardless of how strong our will is. And every instance in which we apply our futile force can result in a conflict that could easily have been avoided. Nothing is ever gained when we create a conflict, even when we think our cause is justified. We have to constantly remember to ask ourselves, "What would God have me do in this instance?"—and then willingly do it.

Being adversarial can become habitual. However, being one who favors compromise can become habitual too.

19.
When you cease to make a contribution, you begin to die.
—Eleanor Roosevelt

The importance of our making an ongoing difference in the lives of others can't be overestimated. We simply must be present in a full and meaningful way to those who find their way onto the path we are traveling. They come with open minds and hearts, and they often possess an inner knowing that we have something to share with them that their own journey needs if it is to continue in its appointed way. There are no mistaken intersections with others. Each person has a contribution to make each time we meet.

Being willing to embrace this idea helps us continue the journey we are making, a journey that is rich with purpose. Having a sure purpose, even though we might not always be able to define exactly what it is, is what gets us out of bed every day. We can always feel that inner pull. And we subtly know both when we touch and are touched by those others with us on our way. The beat goes on; the rhythm of our spiritual evolution never ceases.

Fortunately, we have all been called to make a contribution to life. On those days when someone seems at a loss, if we simply offer the hand of kindness, our purpose will be fulfilled.

20.
Time is a very precious gift of God; so precious
that it's only given to us moment by moment.
—Amelia Barr

What a true blessing it is that life comes to us in tiny increments. Each increment is cradled in the hand of God. No instant is lived alone. God is always present; however, we need to ask for His help. It will never be denied, and He does always know the kind of help we need. But it still falls on us to seek that help. Our relationship with God, not unlike a relationship with a dear friend, merits careful cultivation. He will never reject us. He will always respond lovingly. But we need to fulfill our part of the friendship.

What does it mean to be God's friend? It's my understanding that being His friend means having long chats about whatever is on our mind. It has no particular parameters. He is just *there* to hear us out. He is just *there* to soften whatever blows we might be experiencing. He is *there* to say "Yes" when we need his encouragement to move forward. He is just *there*.

Having a friend like God makes us very lucky people. Never walking through any moment alone is the gift we may never have expected.

21.
What do we live for, if it is not to make life less difficult for each other?
—George Eliot

Choosing to be helpful in our wanderings through life is not only virtuous, it's also far less complicated than the alternative. It relieves us of the decision about how to respond to any experience or to any person whom we encounter. Beginning every day with the commitment to simply be helpful eliminates any hand-wringing as to the proper action to take at any juncture. We are helpful in every instance. Period. And everyone benefits.

Making life easier for others makes life easier for us as well. We can glide through each day knowing how we are going to respond to any situation before it has even occurred. With no need to spend time discerning what the best thing to do is, we can just decide to help instead, which eases the journey for everyone. What a worthy choice.

Today will offer us many opportunities to respond to others. The best choice is to be helpful. If even a few of us did this every day, the world would begin to change in a very positive way.

22.
We are all diamonds in the rough.
—Roseanne Lloyd

That's actually the good news. It means we will be given every opportunity we need to smooth our rough edges. Most often such opportunities come in the form of tough situations and difficult people. But every so often, the wise ones we walk with remind us that God never gives us more than we can handle. And when it feels like the load is too heavy, it probably means we haven't asked for the help He is so willing to give.

Just knowing that our experiences are designed for us personally—that they will indeed help us to shine like the diamonds we are—is worth smiling over. We really don't need to worry about anything. All is in good order, and there is nothing that comes our way that we can't handle with God in our corner. Knowing that we can walk through life relaxed and certain of our destination, even though we might not be able to describe its exact location, is comforting.

Today's experiences will fit our needs perfectly. We are on a specific trajectory, and today is part of the full picture of our lives.

23.
Let each look to himself and see what God wants of
him and attend to this, leaving all else alone.
—Henry Suso

Coming to believe that each one of us has a particular purpose in this life, a purpose quite unlike any other person's, gives us both solace and hope for the day arising before us. We won't really be at a loss about what to do if we go within and check out our "assignment" with the One who knows all things. He never leaves our side, nor will He fail to answer our call for help.

Being reminded that every one of us is necessary to the completion of God and the world we are sharing with each other alleviates any sense of despair we may be harboring regarding our place in this world. We each have a place, and it cannot be filled by anyone else. Cherishing this idea allows for true peace of mind—a deeper peace than we may have felt heretofore. All is well and will always be.

Greeting each day with the knowledge that we have been chosen for our own specific task provides the kind of comfort that most of us seek. Today's task is ours and no one else's.

24.

Pain and chaos in my life give me a chance for transformation.
—Carlotta Posz

Growth and transformation travel hand in glove, and chaos, which is embedded in the many painful situations we experience, can initiate transformations we didn't even realize were on our horizon. Chaos comes our way as we are made ready for it; there is an order to the events in our lives. However, we are not privy to that order ahead of time. The best we can do is understand that what transpires will fit snugly into the sequence of our life's events.

If we could rise above the full picture of our lives and see how all the events have so beautifully knit themselves together, and if we could catch even a glimpse of those which are to come, we'd be completely at peace. We have woven a beautiful tapestry combining all the colorful events of our lives, and the tapestry's full beauty has yet to be revealed in its completeness.

The opportunity for growth that presents itself today is another beautiful thread in the tapestry of our lives. Be grateful for it. We aren't done yet.

25.

Looking for good in other people improves our attitude.

How simple and yet profound this idea is. Changing our minds about how we see another person is the single most important decision we can make when we are harboring negative judgments.

EACH DAY A RENEWED BEGINNING

Seeking to see the good which is always there instead inspires us to see the good in ourselves as well. What we see in others is generally a reflection of how we see ourselves. If we are focused on the negative within, we need to search our minds to see the negatives that we have projected onto whomever stands before us.

Who we see is who we are! That's not an easy idea to integrate into our understanding. We generally don't want to admit that we have all of the negative traits that we project onto others. Seeing them there allows us to feel superior in the moment, but in the final analysis, feeling superior is a double-edged sword. We aren't superior. And on top of that, our judgment makes us feel ashamed.

A good attitude is a direct result of having a good opinion of all the others who travel with us. Remembering that each one of them is special to our journey can help us to rapidly refocus how we see them.

Today is full of promise. What I do with it is up to me.

26.
The most important thing I learned in life was the value of getting along with others.
— Pat Jerome

Choosing to get along with others is a decision. It's not always easy either. It's a fact that some people are simply easier to be around. Perhaps it's because they are peaceful, or perhaps it's because we are more willing to let them show up on our path however they choose to without our interference. The desire to change others to fit our needs and expectations can be strong and can cause trouble for all concerned.

Because we need to get along with others at home, in our neighborhoods, and in our workplaces, making a decision every day to let go when it comes to circumstances involving others makes our own journeys so much more peaceful. It's really not very difficult once we have committed to trying it. In fact, it makes our own lives far simpler when we learn to back off—to surrender to what is—rather than trying to make others change to be who we want them to be.

Today is a good day to practice backing off and letting others live free of our interference. It's truly not all that hard.

27.

Example is the lesson that all men can read.
—Gilbert West

Being an example of good for all those with whom we travel is the loving choice that God wants us to make. Not very much is asked of any of us, but acting from a place of kindness comes quickly to mind. I'm convinced that's all God hopes for from each one of us. The simplest response is to decide that kindness will always be how we respond. By taking the guesswork out of our decisions, making this choice simplifies our lives. But even better, it makes our lives far more peaceful and can cause those we touch to feel the hand of peace as well.

Setting the intention to be a good example for others today is an easy choice. And even better, it's one that will have a positive impact on a multitude of people.

28.

Do not let the behavior of others destroy your inner peace.
—The Dalai Lama

It's not always easy to detach from the behavior of others when they are intent on acting out, but if we want inner peace, we have the choice to step aside. This is a habit we can hone, as a matter of fact. Many of us often find ourselves in the midst of folks we'd rather avoid but for the fact that life has given us other opportunities. It's well to remember that someone else's behavior is the very trigger we might need to be who we are being called to be.

With God's help, all things can be for our good. We can quit fretting from this moment on. Whatever or whoever seems to be troubling us, it has already been dealt with in the most perfect way. God is always present and part of every solution. And lest we forget, whoever does seemingly destroy our peace of mind has arrived right on time. All is in divine order, now and always.

We can breathe a big sigh of relief today. God is present to handle whatever surfaces. We face nothing alone.

29.
Each day is different and has a surprise in it, like a Cracker Jack box.
—Alpha English

Comparing the coming day to a Cracker Jack box is certainly a refreshing way to prepare for whatever lies ahead. Every day will offer us many exciting experiences. The comforting realization is that with God as our companion, nothing we face will be really scary because He is walking us through it. As a matter of fact, nothing is truly unexpected either. We may not know what's coming down the pike, but our Higher Self is always aware of what's just around the corner, and we have been prepared for what is to come by all of our preceding experiences.

Our lives are unfolding perfectly. That may not be an easy idea to adopt wholeheartedly, particularly if we just lost a job or a relationship is beginning to sour. But what is happening at any particular moment in our lives is on target. If we could only come to fully believe that, our journeys would be so much easier to understand and accept. Try for now to believe that nothing has happened or will ever happen that isn't part of the perfect plan for our lives. With that belief, we will be filled with peace.

We deserve peace. And every day we can expect peace. We simply have to remember that nothing is coming our way that hasn't been planned for.

30.
Actions speak louder than words. You show love by everything that you do.
—Violet Hensley

If only we could remember to pause long enough to monitor our own behavior before we let it take us someplace that we don't want to go. Few of us set out to hurt others, and most of us believe in the principle that what we do to others comes back to us, sometimes swiftly, sometimes when we least expect it. But it will return. That in itself should be reminder enough to give only love to all of those who visit our path on any given day.

No doubt most of us closely watch the behavior of others. And we take note of those actions that are kind, the small gestures that make others feel noticed and cherished. We are also aware of bullies in our midst who try to make others feel insignificant or unworthy. As onlookers, we know who we want to emulate; yet there are times when we fail to respond in a loving way to someone crossing our path. But we can change. We *can* change.

Today will be full of opportunities to give love to others. However, we are in the driver's seat. The choice to act lovingly is one we must make.

31.

Taking an inventory of our behavior at the end of the day is a great first step to changing those behaviors that aren't pleasing to God.

Paying close attention to who we have been in the preceding few hours is the only honest way we can reel in those behaviors that don't fill us with pride. And it's a great habit to develop. It takes only a few moments before falling asleep to review how the day went. Experiences that weren't handled in the best possible way will come to mind ever so quickly. Amends, if called for, can be made the next day so that each day can then go on with a clean slate.

Not carrying all of our transgressions around day after day frees us to become the better self we all hope to become. Within each of us is a better example of who we could be than what we may show others on a moment's notice. Sometimes we are simply caught off guard and act or speak too quickly, falling short of the person we'd really rather be. But we always have a second chance. That's the good news about striving to live more consciously.

Knowing what we could have done better yesterday can help us act from a higher plane today. Inventories serve us and our companions well.

AUGUST

————————— 1. —————————

**Not every lesson that we are invited to learn feels good;
however, nary a one of them is superfluous to our journey.**

That painful experiences in life are as important to our growth as
the easy experiences isn't what we want to hear. But we have all
heard the saying, "No pain, no gain," and unfortunately, it has a
ring of truth to it. Does an experience have to be painful to teach
us something? Of course not. But we can't just run from one that is
distressing, hoping it will become something else. If an unpleasant
happening has paid a visit, we needed the experience to prepare us
for the next stage of who we are becoming.

Our lives are not static, thank goodness. There are those days when
we want to pull the blankets over our heads and say, "Not now,"
but the option to close the world out isn't one we can fully espouse,
not if we want to become the people we were born to be. We do all
have a specific task in this life, and no two of us have been created
for the same one. If we can embrace the power of this idea even for
a moment, we will get a sense of how awesome our journey really is.

*Whatever gets our attention today has come on cue. We may not like the
experience, but let's try to remember we need it for the journey we have been
called to make.*

————————— 2. —————————

**Hope arouses, as nothing else can arouse,
a passion for the possible.
—William Sloane Coffin Jr.**

Walking into my first 12-step meeting changed my life in a
profound way. It was in 1974, and it was an Al-Anon meeting. I
experienced hope for a changed life within moments of being there
that night. The change I felt was immediate and intense; I had felt
bereft of hope prior to that fateful night. I left the meeting knowing
that I could survive, that I could eventually do what all of these

other individuals were doing. Did I know how? Not at all; but the feeling I left with was palpable. I knew I had to go back.

The experience of hope, regardless of the circumstance that inspires it, changes us profoundly. It energizes our minds and our movements. It is the seed for change of any kind, and once the seed is planted, it begins to germinate. What comes next depends of course on the individual and the circumstance, but change will transpire. And growth, or peace of mind, or both, are guaranteed. Hope is truly the first step to the manifestation of whatever we deeply desire.

Hope is an elixir. It creates a different mood, and we are changed, perhaps forever. Let's seek to recognize the hopeful circumstances in our lives today.

3.
Some things we think are bad may be good.
—Harry Bartholomew

It's never wise to assume we understand the full impact of a circumstance until we see what it has wrought. How many times have we come to realize that the worst thing that could possibly have happened was, in retrospect, what opened the door to opportunities far beyond our imagination? When my first husband sought a divorce, I was devastated. His infidelities had been crushing blows, but I wasn't eager to be alone, regardless. However, had he not left, the myriad experiences that ultimately led me into the rooms of recovery as well as graduate school would perhaps not have transpired.

I have come to believe that whatever does happen in our lives is the perfect occurrence at that point in time. Without each life event, no one reading this book would be where he or she is right now. And we can be grateful that everything visits us at the perfect time. Our lives are a composite of all experiences, all encounters, all disappointments and joys. With gratitude, recognize this will always be true.

This day will be exactly what it needs to be. We will be introduced to the experiences we have been made ready for. And all of them will be for our ultimate good.

4.

Life is an adventure in forgiveness.
—Norman Cousins

For certain, life is an adventure. But thinking of it as an adventure in *forgiveness* creates a whole new direction for us to go. It surely suggests that we might be up to our necks in difficult experiences, at least part of each day. And while that might concern us at first glance, we can choose to see this as the very collection of life experiences we chose for ourselves. And this is of course absolutely true. Whatever comes our way was on our radar, by choice, long before it made its appearance. It's not unusual that we may have forgotten it. In fact, that's quite likely. But responding lovingly to every experience is truly living the gift of forgiveness.

Forgiveness of others and ourselves is the invitation to connection we all so clearly crave, in fact. Forgiveness is the healing balm that every soul seeks. To know that every day will offer us an opportunity to experience this kind of healing takes the sting out of any unappreciated experience. Each event has its perfect part in our story.

Today will be an adventure, and some experiences may arise that invite us to be forgiving. Be grateful for them. They draw us closer to one another.

5.

The deepest principle in human nature is
the craving to be appreciated.
—William James

Initially we may resist believing this idea. Doesn't it make us sound too clingy and codependent? Perhaps that's one way to interpret James' idea, but I'm inclined to think that wasn't his intention at all; rather he was suggesting we make an expression of kindness wherever possible. And indeed, we do all seek to be treated kindly. Others obviously deserve the same from us.

Taking this idea and acting on it as often as possible could change the vibration of the universe. Lives would change worldwide if every person treated even one or two people with kindness every day, and they, in turn, passed that kindness on to others as well. Perhaps it seems farfetched to think we could have an impact on the whole planet by simply choosing kindness in a few encounters, but indeed, we can—and should.

Today is as good a day as any to make a commitment to being truly helpful and kind, wherever we go. Everyone we meet will be a lucky recipient, and we will feel better too.

6.

Would you rather be cursing the darkness or lighting the candles?
—Connie Hilliard

We are far too familiar with individuals who always see the negative side of everything that is happening or even has the potential to happen. They are not much fun to be around, and unfortunately, they are often folks we are forced to be with, whether on the job or in social settings that we can't easily avoid. But there are the bright lights too, and we are so drawn to them. When these two kinds of people are present at the same gathering, it's interesting to see how the rest of the guests align themselves. It's been my experience that those who see the glass as half full tend to have far more people in their circle of listeners.

What is it that initiates this negativity in some people? Surely they aren't born with it—or are they? Perhaps being negative provides some payoff that is its own reward. Negative people seldom change, and it's just as common that positive people generally remain that way all their lives as well. How fortunate for the rest of us that we have the option, in every setting, to sidle up to those who foster joy.

Making the choice to be positive rather than negative may not come automatically, but we can practice it. We will feel far better if we do.

7.

Example moves the world more than doctrine.
—Henry Miller

Whether we are aware of it or not, every action we take shows someone else who we are, at least in that moment. Being cognizant of that can help us curtail our own behaviors that do not fill us with pride. We all have them. We are human and fallible, after all. But showing up as our better selves is always an option. We simply have to know who that better self is.

Every day, we can observe our fellow travelers, including some whom we admire for their actions and, of course, some we don't. We can learn from their example, and we can if we choose set a positive example for others. The choice to model good behavior isn't a difficult one really, but it is one that requires intention and commitment. No bad habit is changed easily. But new and better habits can become second nature with practice.

Today is a day that will afford us many opportunities to practice being the person we'd rather be and to bless the planet many times over.

8.

I am here only to be truly helpful; I am here
to represent Him who sent me.
—A Course in Miracles

We do all have a specific purpose in this life, one that is larger than ourselves. For some, it's to lead a great organization. For others, it's to teach children how to function in a quickly changing world. Caring for the sick is a calling perhaps unmatched in its heroism, particularly in this time of rampantly spreading COVID-19. But for anyone who is uncertain and searching for direction, tuning into the idea of simply being truly helpful is a purpose that is both huge and completely fulfilling.

Mother Teresa lived so intentionally, thereby making life better for thousands of others, all by just loving each one in even a very small way. She was known to have said, "Be kind to everyone, and start with the person standing next to you." What a beautiful standard to live up to. And not one that's beyond any one of us. The decision to do so is all that's required.

Today stands before us like an unopened envelope. Let's greet the contents both humbly and lovingly.

9.

What God arranges for us to experience at each moment is the best and holiest thing that could happen.
— Jean-Pierre de Caussade

What a comforting idea this is. We are getting the best in each instant because of God's unwavering love. What we must grow to understand and appreciate, however, is that not every example of God's love may feel comforting when first experienced. I can certainly look back on my life and remember times that were jarring and unanticipated and which hurt greatly at the time, for instance, when my first husband chose to leave me for another woman. And yet, God was opening the door to a far better life for me. Sometimes pain is a precursor to the next holy gift.

What happened for me as a result of that deeply troubling rejection was a life beyond my wildest imagination. I would never have guessed I would get a PhD. I also never would have guessed my alcoholism would lead me into a fulfilling life as a writer. When my husband left, I was devastated. But God had another plan for me all along, and this will always be the truth of our lives.

Whatever is on our horizon today is coming wrapped in the loving care of God.

10.

Do the best you can until you know better.
Then when you know better, do better.
— Maya Angelou

We tend to complicate our lives needlessly. The formula for living a good life is to do good things for others. Being truly helpful to at least one other person every day is not beyond our ability by any stretch of the imagination. It may be beyond our willingness, however, and when that's the case, it's our own lives that are shortchanged. Doing something helpful or kind for even one other person actually helps two people in the same moment.

The peace of mind that comes over us when we have given our best in any single moment is almost indescribable. Receiving the gift of peace due to a simple action we chose to take makes us want to do them on a regular basis, and then people around us are blessed by every one of them. But the blessing doesn't end there. Any person who has felt that hand of goodness is inclined to offer a moment of kindness to someone else as well. In due time, the shift toward kindness is felt everywhere.

We can be a part of the change that is needed throughout the world today. All it takes is an act of goodness on our part.

11.

What you do makes a difference, and you have to decide what kind of difference you want to make.
— Jane Goodall

Jane Goodall is still making a difference in the lives of gorillas. Her compassionate humanity toward them is representative of her humanity toward all life. She provides an excellent role model to all of us of what love looks like. Her commitment to the gorillas began when she was in her youth, and she has been unwavering ever since. Few individuals can be pointed to in the course of history who have remained strong and resolute for a lifetime.

I think the lesson for all of us is that while we don't all have to be Jane Goodalls, we can still make a difference that registers for a lifetime if we seek to bring our own love and humanity to a cause that's worthy of our attention. It doesn't need to be a big cause either. A tiny one will do. And the tiniest one I can think of is smiling kindly with our eyes, behind our masks, when we greet others on the street or in the grocery. Tipping our head to say hello, "I see you and acknowledge you," is a tiny gesture that makes

a difference, as important a difference as what Jane Goodall is
still doing.

*Being intentional in how we wander through life today, being examples of love
and peace, will make the kind of difference our friends, colleagues, and even
complete strangers need.*

12.
**When we are no longer able to change a situation,
we are challenged to change ourselves.**
—Viktor E. Frankl

The good news is that we never have the absolute power to change
either any situation or any person, only the part we play in the
experience or relationship. Indeed, if we had the power to change
everything we encounter, our lives would be overwhelmed by angst
and tension. Seldom would we feel the gift of a peaceful heart or
mind. But we can experience both on a regular basis when we
finally understand that our powers are limited to our own lives
only—and that's a good thing.

We will move through every day meeting up with the people
and situations that are right for our growth in this moment in
time, yet nary a one of them needs our absolute control, only our
acceptance. No one else's life is our "assignment." And no specific
situation is presented to us for our sole dedication or resolution.
We are "parties" to all that comes our way. We are sharing the
experience—always.

*How lucky we are if we have come to appreciate our freedom from trying to
control the uncontrollable. Today is only for our blessing and our joy.*

13.
**It is what we all do with our hearts that
affects others most deeply.**
—Gerald Jampolsky

Opening our hearts to others changes them and us from that
moment forward. But what does it mean to open our hearts? This

can perhaps be interpreted in many ways, but I think it means being truly vulnerable with and accepting of others as they are and loving them fully, with no judgments or criticisms. All people yearn for is to be themselves. For us to put restrictions on what we expect others to do in order to be loved is to close our hearts to their humanity.

Our lives here on this planet are exceedingly short. To cheat ourselves and others of the full expression of our love is cutting short the blessings of each moment. They are always present, but we have to acknowledge them to make them real. Time may be running out; we never know when our journey is nearing the end. Not opening our hearts wholeheartedly to all those who are journeying with us is shortchanging ourselves and everyone else too. Remember, no one has come our way unbidden.

Meeting others with our hearts open is all that God wants from us. Dedicating ourselves to doing so is a decision that once made, will lighten our hearts.

14.
To stop behaving in a certain way is to risk the unfamiliar.
— Jan Lloyd

Habits are comfortable. Unfortunately, even bad habits can be as comfortable as an old pair of shoes, and making the decision to change any habit takes willingness. Developing that willingness often requires serious consideration of who we'd rather be in these ever-so-common situations when our bad habits surface.

We may have very little familiarity with new, untried behaviors, so embarking on changing an old behavior pattern can cause us to feel unsettled initially. It's only after consistently implementing an unfamiliar behavior that it will start to feel better to us than one we practiced in the past. The positive realization that supports this process is that we begin to like the person we are becoming. It begins to feel far better to behave in ways that gain approval from others. Even though other people may not have criticized all of our bad habits, we were woefully aware of them.

Everyone gains when we decide to change a bad habit. Today may well give us an opportunity to review one that could be changed. Don't duck it.

15.

If one is going to be truthful, one has to be very tender.
—Florida Scott-Maxwell

We have been told since childhood that we should tell the truth. And we know from our own experiences that when we do tell the truth, we are relieved of the burden of worrying about what story we told and to whom. Living by and with the truth is far easier on our minds and hearts. However, the words we use to tell the truth are key. It should never be our intent to hurt someone with the truth. It therefore comes down to the selection of the words we use, coupled with our tone of voice.

Being truthful in our responses to others is always easier on our own minds, and if we choose to speak the truth thoughtfully and lovingly, we will not be as likely to hurt the feelings of others. The bottom line is the same in all conversations: speak the truth, but speak it with compassion and awareness about how your words will be heard by others. We only "come around once" in life. Let's be a blessing in all instances with every word we choose to share.

Telling the truth never has to be harsh. Tell it in the way you'd like to hear it. You will have an opportunity today.

16.

I don't think we're in charge of our lives.
For this I thank God all the time.
—Janice Clark

Being reminded that we are not in charge of our lives offers us well deserved freedom. Since God is in charge, all we need do is listen for divine guidance and then follow through. Life is far less complicated when we "let go and let God," as the saying goes. We will never be led astray. There will be times when we may think God has let us down; however, His plans always right-size us and bring us to where we need to be, moment by moment.

We may not initially see where God's plan is taking us. In fact, quite often that will be the case. But we will grow in our willingness to trust His guidance when we revisit where it has carried us in the past. He will never take us where harm will befall us. Our resistance to where his guidance has led us may result in confusion or worse, but we will always be led to where the perfect lessons are waiting for us. God can always be trusted. Hindsight confirms this.

Greeting each day in the knowledge that God is in charge makes it easier to breathe more freely. We will never be in doubt about what to do today. Just listen.

17.
Your body is not who you are. The mind and spirit transcend the body.
—Christopher Reeve

Reeve's life was dramatically changed in 1995 when he was thrown from a horse. Amazingly, his paralysis didn't define him. He knew he was far more than a body, and he shifted his focus to his spiritual center. Fortunately, we need not experience paralysis to make the same discovery. What's far more real about us is our mind and the spirit that is ever present to guide us. If you are ever confused about the truth of this idea, remember that bodies aren't eternal. They serve us, and then we lay them aside.

Spirit is how we connect to the voice of God that is forever present to guide and care for us throughout this journey. Reeve's journey was far from over when he had the accident. He simply came into awareness of what his real journey was about. We can all connect with the deeper reality of that journey if we choose to do so. It will always be present, and hopefully, when we are open to it, we will acknowledge it.

Today will offer at least one more opportunity to discover the real purpose of our journey here. Listen, and you will hear spirit call.

18.

Why should I let him decide what kind of day I'm going to have?
— Sidney Harris

Perhaps no wiser words have ever been said. We are too easily ensnared by what others are doing or saying, and whatever peace we might have been feeling may then be snatched from us. But we can learn to detach from the behavior of others. Admittedly, it's not easy the first time we try it, but when we decide that we are no longer willing to give up who we want to be, we can more comfortably turn away. Turning away doesn't mean we have to discard those people from our lives. But we each have a right to remain unaffected by whatever means it takes.

We have to value ourselves enough to make the choice to turn away when others are interfering with our peace of mind, sometimes even going so far as leaving the room. Not everyone acting out is trying to get under our skin, but the decision always rests with us as to how we want to handle it. No words even have to be spoken.

Almost every day we find ourselves in situations where someone else's behavior disturbs us. Never forget, we are in charge of our reactions in every instance.

19.

You find peace not by rearranging the circumstances of your life, but by realizing who you are at the deepest level.
— Eckhart Tolle

At our very core, we are peace. In that deepest of all inner spaces, the rhythm of our life is quiet and connected to the Source who provides us with the peace we yearn for. Because of all the stimuli grabbing for our attention, we seldom go deep enough inside to realize that sought-for serenity is there. Instead, we let the ever-changing circumstances around us interfere with our state of being, and the peace we seek slips further away. It never leaves, however — never. It's who we are.

The constant distractions surrounding us make it difficult to fully embrace the peace that waits for us within. What we are guaranteed, however, is that we will never seek for it in vain. No distraction can hold us for long if we desire freedom from it for even a moment. It's our call. What do we want? The outer world of disruption and dis-ease, or the inner experience of heavenly peace? We get to choose.

We are offered this choice every moment of this day: Do you want peace or its absence? Choose wisely.

20.

We cannot always oblige, but we can always speak obligingly.
—Voltaire

How we interact with our fellow man is what defines us as a person. We can always choose to be an expression of love. Doing so nourishes the gentle rhythm at the heart of the universe we share. We have such power in each moment to direct the flow of every encounter that we experience. If we do not take our responsibility for making this universe a better place for us all seriously, we are passing up the opportunity to be the blessing we were born to be. Let's not forget that God is our companion in every encounter.

We often make our lives far more stressful than they need to be. We may misinterpret comments as criticisms, and our ego may react when acceptance or detachment would be a far better response. Setting forth each day with the intention of bringing our better selves along in every conversation assuredly changes how we feel at the end of the day. We can always be kind. Period.

We can give ourselves the break we deserve today and keep life simple. Be loving, regardless of the circumstances.

21.

To love is to allow another person to be whomever they are without making an attempt to change them.
—Anonymous

Far too seldom do we let this way of loving serve as our guide. Just tweaking the other person a bit here and there is so much more common as well as seductive. Unfortunately, on occasion they do change and become a bit more like we'd hoped they'd be, and then we are convinced it's because of our tweaking. Thus, the madness continues. What we must realize, and even appreciate, is that we have no control over someone else's behavior — not ever. If they change, it's solely because they have made a different choice about their own behavior.

If we were actually powerful enough to control the behavior of someone else, the burden would be heavy indeed. Our own lives would suffer from inattention, and we'd find ourselves on an emotional rollercoaster much of the time. Just having our own selves and our own lives to control is a big job, particularly if we are attentively responding to all the opportunities to be our better selves that come our way every day.

Showing up in each experience as a loving presence is exactly what God hopes we will do. And the more we can fulfill that hope, the greater will be our peace of mind.

22.

If you are depressed, you are living in the past.
If you are anxious, you are living in the future;
if you are at peace, you are living in the present.
— Junia Bretas

We so easily can get sucked into thoughts of the past or fears about the future. It's almost as though our minds set out to sabotage us. Why is connecting to this moment, the only moment we really have, so difficult? It comes from lack of discipline, I think. We lazily allow our minds to meander wherever they have a habit of going instead of being awed by the moment. It's within each moment as it's being lived that God is saying, "Here I am." And in that assurance, peace is the unending gift.

The past has nothing to offer us except the occasional good memory. However, we will miss making more good memories if we let this moment standing before us slip away. And incessant worry about the future never makes a space for the presence of God right now. This moment, *now*, is where our real gifts reside. And in this moment, there is nothing to worry about — not ever. Let's not turn away from it.

Today is a panoply of moments, each one more precious than the last. Let not a single one be lost because of a mind that wanders. Remember, now is all there is.

23.
Let God love you through others, and let
God love others through you.
— D. M. Street

The key of course is God. He is everywhere, in everyone, and always present as the pathway to love and connection. And if we seek to see Him in everyone, we will experience the comfort we yearn for. The question is, how do we experience God's love from others? The answer is simple. Take note of them from our own loving perspective, and we will see only love in their very being. We will always see that which we project — always.

Likewise, to pass God's love on to others is simple too: be attentive, be kind, be accepting, be truly helpful in every instance. Those we journey with will feel God's love every time we cross paths. To give and receive God's love is really one and the same. What we give returns to us tenfold. Making the choice to always let it be love can be a decision we make one time, for good.

God is, and all is well. That's all we really need to remember to be at peace.

24.
It is good to have an end to journey towards; but
it is the journey that matters, in the end.
— Ursula K. LeGuin

For most of our lives, we have been encouraged to set goals. There are workshops galore with the specific theme of goal setting, how to write them, and, even more importantly, how to determine the steps to accomplish them. Having a goal isn't foolhardy; on the contrary, it serves an important purpose. It gets us out of bed in the morning and is often the driving force behind our activities all day long. However, it's the activities themselves that really matter. They provide the richness that makes the journey itself exciting and fulfilling.

In actuality, both the goal *and* the journey keep us on course and help us fulfill the purpose for which we are here. The idea for a goal is, after all, God inspired. We may not realize that when the seed of a goal is being planted in our minds, but with hindsight, we will come to understand its source. God is the ever-present guide in all our affairs, including our journey, from beginning to end.

We need not fret about successfully completing a goal. God, who inspires our goals, is walking every step of the way with us to complete it. Peace is ours.

25.
The absence of love in our lives is what makes
them seem raw and unfinished.
— Ingrid Bengis

It's important that we know love isn't really ever absent from our lives. Because we are imbued with the presence of God, we are likewise filled to overflowing with His love. There are those who think God is the presence of unconditional love in our lives; count me among them. Wherever we go, love goes with us. If we feel raw and unfinished, it's because we have forgotten that God goes everywhere with us. In fact, we can't go anywhere without God. He is with us whether we acknowledge Him or not.

To feel raw and unfinished is the ego at work; it always wants us to be unsure of ourselves. It isn't our friend, I assure you. It's the voice in our minds that speaks first and loudest, yet its message is always wrong. But because it is so insistent and feels just as present as God, we have to be fiercely committed to God so we aren't thrown off course. Making the decision to pause as we are listening to the voice in our mind, and then deciding to follow only the gentle guidance of the softer inner voice, means we will never feel raw and unfinished. The choice is ours.

Today will be as comforting as we allow it to be. The decision of which voice will guide us is ours, every moment of the day.

26.

When we can harmonize our personal desires with God's larger plan for us, we find true pleasure.
—Dorothy Pierson

We often find ourselves in a position where we want something specific yet seem unable to make it happen. Our frustration is great at those times, and it is seldom that we remember in the midst of the struggle that God simply has a better plan for us. Too often we feel certain, even absolutely certain, that what we want is right for us. The fact that the door to what we desire won't open is maddening; yet, with hindsight, we can see how much better God's plan was all along.

Will we ever finally learn that God is the guide to the better plan in every instance? We are never truly on our own. We can certainly act against God's plan, and we sometimes do, but those outcomes are generally unsatisfactory. It's not that God doesn't allow us to act against His will, but fortunately the consequences of doing so will likely change our outlook in time. Deciding God is a far better life planner than our own limited consciousness makes living so much easier.

God does have a plan for today. Let's celebrate it.

27.

Hesitation is the best cure for anger.
—Seneca

The wisdom contained in these few words can be life-changing. Taking a moment to think before reacting, perhaps saying a prayer or even just pausing long enough to count to five, can change the tenor of a relationship in a moment. We have all been guilty of reacting too quickly to a situation or another person's comment far too often. Why is it so hard to choose to be quiet?

Actually, I'm not so sure it *is* hard. It's just an unpracticed choice, but we can begin making this our more frequent choice from this moment forward. We can't expect others to change how they choose to behave, but we can make the decision to change ourselves. Learning as we can and must that no one else's mood has the power to determine who we will be changes our lives in exponentially positive ways.

Today is a new day, and it will offer many opportunities to take charge of our own moods, rather than allowing someone else to control them.

28.

It is now clear to me that from the beginning, some human beings saw that the best way to take life was lightly.
—Florida Scott-Maxwell

The wisdom of taking life lightly can't be overestimated. It is so common to respond too quickly to situations, even before we have considered what they really mean. Pausing for even a minute or two can give us the break we need, and, in the meantime, the situation can change dramatically. Most experiences do not call for immediate responses. In fact, many experiences call for no response at all.

Knowing when to respond and when to remain quiet is the mark of true wisdom. A shrug of the shoulders may well be one of the smartest responses we can make to any situation we encounter today. How many times have we overreacted to something, only to feel foolish when we saw what the real story was? We can live life far more simply—beginning today.

It's not a difficult decision, really, to say nothing when confronted by any kind of situation. Staying quiet allows us the time to see what's really there to see.

29.

Someone else's mood need not control our own.

Being able to step aside from someone else's ugly mood isn't all that easy. But with enough practice, it can become a habit. Some people exist in relationships where strife is common; alcoholism is at the root of many troubled relationships. Mental illness can cause constant eruptions in families too, particularly if left untreated. And in all of these instances, plus many more, staying grounded in the practice of not responding to angry outbursts often takes Herculean effort. We often think: Why me? Why do I have to figure out how to live with this? Why shouldn't he or she be the one to change?

And while our feelings may well be justified, the fact remains that we can put a stop to having our moods so easily hijacked. We have the power to detach from the words and actions of others, regardless of what they are. We may have to leave the room, or even the house, but we can remove ourselves and seek quiet refuge. In the quiet, we can know peace even when all around us is a storm of negativity.

Every day, some situation or person is likely to ensnare our peace of mind. Fortunately, by removing ourselves from the circumstance, we can always reclaim it.

30.
Sometimes the worst things that happen to us are the best things for us.
—Alice Merryman

In the midst of a really uncomfortable experience, we are probably hard pressed to think, "Gee, this is good." But in hindsight, we have all learned so much over the years. When something unthinkable happened, doors opened that we might never have walked through otherwise. I think what's key is trusting that God is always present to help us navigate the rough waters that can be stirred up by any unexpected situation.

Deciding to rejoice in every experience that comes our way is how we can respond favorably to the everyday gifts God is constantly giving us. We never ever encounter any new experience alone; God is always with us, front and center. Even if we don't feel His presence, He's there. We can't escape Him! Getting in touch with the truth of this significantly changes our lives. Worrying can become a thing of the past.

Each day we awake to new opportunities for experiencing God's presence, and each one of them is perfect for who we have become at this moment in time.

31.

A complete revaluation takes place in your physical and mental being when you've laughed and had some fun.
— Catherine Ponder

Laughter changes our outlook, some would say even our very being. In fact, Norman Cousins, a famous political journalist, wrote a book about self-healing a number of years ago where he described his own process of healing through watching funny movies and massive infusions of vitamin C. He was a strong adherent of the philosophy that laughter has healing power because of its effect on the adrenal system. It does for sure have the power to change our attitudes in the moment, and the accumulation of many moments with a good attitude does change the very tenor of our lives.

I don't think, however, that we need to sit for hours and watch Groucho Marx. But deciding to take situations more lightly can get the ball rolling. No one is in charge of our moods but ourselves. And lest I be misunderstood, a serious mood isn't a bad thing. There is a time and a place for that. But we yearn to live more peacefully, and seeing the softer side of life can give us that freedom. It's hard to be at peace if we are always in the stranglehold of a serious state of mind.

Today will be filled with possibilities for laughter. Don't fail to relish every one of them.

SEPTEMBER

1.

**"I can forgive but I cannot forget" is only
another way of saying "I cannot forgive."
—Henry Ward Beecher**

It's a pretty well-established fact that holding onto resentments makes being at peace nearly impossible. Resentments have a way of sabotaging our well-being. They consume us, and when our minds are held hostage by such feelings, peace is only a distant memory. But there is a way to live free of the turmoil in our minds; we can achieve this by letting go of our resentments and then coupling that with the actual decision to forgive whomever we have allowed to steal our peace of mind.

Forgiveness is the purest form of connection to someone else. And when it's heartfelt, it's absolutely mind-altering. It is said that the joining of two minds in the act of forgiveness becomes the holiest place on earth. All angst is gone, all tension released. All resistance to the person standing before us melts away. We can then move forward peacefully and gratefully. The added blessing is that all other relationships are made more loving too.

If there is someone who needs forgiveness today, don't tarry. The blessing will be felt immediately.

2.

**The tragedy of disliking a fellow is that we
want everyone else to dislike him too.
—Frank A. Clark**

How small-minded this statement is, but it is too often true. And it's not just the folks we personally know, but those we see in the media who get under our skin. We want our friends and associates to dislike them as well. When it comes to judgment against others, many of us have a lot of soul-searching to do. Having a poor attitude about any person poisons how we perceive everyone else on our path.

Of course, the converse is true too. Accepting all our fellow travelers, regardless of their opinions, is not only uplifting, it's contagious. The people we meet in life are those who have been chosen to be our teachers. Perhaps the biggest lesson some of us have to learn is tolerance. If we were surrounded only by people we agreed with on everything, we'd be missing out on some important lessons that are key for us to experience on this journey.

What fun today will be if we look upon all our encounters as the opportunities for learning that they really are.

3.

Dare to be empty. Dare to let go. Dare to believe.
—Elizabeth L.

Dare to let God be at the center of your life. Everything about our journey would dramatically change if we were able to empty ourselves of our ego concerns, let go of our need to control, and believe without a shadow of doubt that God is fully present and willing to handle every concern we have. Indeed He is, and this is a truth that will never change.

We really could sail through life without a single worry if we embraced this one simple truth: *God is here now.* And He isn't present just as an onlooker but as the power to guide our every move if we only step aside and let Him. Why do we think we need to be in charge? What gave rise to this folly? Perhaps it grew from one single instance where we mistakenly assumed something had worked out "our way" because of our string-pulling. It's time to give up magical thinking. What has worked out has always had the hand of God in it.

God is present to guide us through whatever we face today. Walk with assurance. All is well.

4.

Today I forgive all those who have ever offended me.
— Paramahansa Yogananda

The willingness to forgive everyone for everything opens the door
to lasting peace of mind. But forgiving absolutely everyone is the
necessary ingredient. Holding off forgiving one or two people
because we think their behavior is egregious is the same as holding
resentments against everyone. We can't freely feel the peace for
which we so yearn if we are holding on to any particular incident
and judging it unforgivable.

It may initially seem impossible to embrace a fully forgiving state
of mind, but we have all been privy to folks who always seem to be
peaceful. Could it be that they freely let others off the hook? Might
their peaceful demeanor be evidence that they hold no resentments
against anyone? Giving this a try, for even a day, might be the best
lesson we will ever experience. Let everything go—just for these
next few hours, as a test.

*This day lying before us is our opportunity to live unfettered by judgment and
resentment. It may seem impossible, but what others can do, we can do too.*

5.

We are who we are, shaped and molded by the times, by
the events, and by the people we encounter on our way.
— Ruth Casey

We must assume that nothing that happens in our midst and no
one who shows up on our path fails to leave their mark. We truly
become a composite of all that we experience. And that means
we must closely monitor all those who wander our way. We don't
necessarily want everyone to make an indelible mark. We can't
completely avoid everyone's impact, but we can step aside from
those individuals we know are out to do us harm emotionally
or physically.

Fortunately, we always have the power to choose the people and
experiences we want to embrace. Likewise, we have the power to

say no to the many negative experiences that flow in our direction. We need not be a sponge for every person and all that comes with them. We do have the power of choice, and that, indeed, makes all the difference in who we are becoming on this journey.

Let's be wary today before we fully take into ourselves what comes our way. We can learn from all experiences, but that doesn't mean we have to let them influence us permanently.

6.
God is always within.

These four words say it all. God has taken up residence within us. That's how close He actually is. When we fully surrender to this knowledge, our lives become easy and oh, so peaceful. We need fight nothing, because nothing comes our way that we, along with God, can't handle. As a matter of fact, it's kind of fun to test this truth. Start taking note of everything that is happening. At first glance, some circumstances may seem to have sticking points, but then, when we surrender them to God, everything changes.

This has been true our entire lives, of course. But many of us didn't realize how present God is. As a result, we complicated our lives. Instead of simply surrendering to His guidance, we struggled to make whatever the situation was work in our favor. The perfect divine outcome was always just waiting for us to invite it into our lives and acknowledge it. God was always there.

How lucky are we. Nothing can stump us. Nothing can hold us hostage. Nothing, that is, as long as we turn everything over to our ever-present helper.

7.
All that is necessary to make this world a better place is to love; to love as Christ loved, to love as Buddha loved.
—Isadora Duncan

Of course, this makes so much sense. To love and be loved unconditionally would make our lives a great deal more certain, not to mention more peaceful. But we have to consider, for a moment, just how unconditionally we love others. Probably few of us can say that we wholeheartedly love our fellow man unconditionally. Most of us can't really even love our dearest friends and family members unconditionally. Too often, there are conditions attached. Usually unspoken, but they are there nonetheless.

We have to be willing to remove all conditions—to surrender to the act of loving others *just because*. No questions raised. No conditions voiced or unvoiced. In fact, no conditions even considered. The best and the worst of someone is loved wholly; only then is the world a better place. Only then are we at peace in this better world. Only then will we have done the part we were born to play.

Our divine assignment is simple: love one another wholly, without conditions.

8.

I know I need something to do every day. It probably doesn't even matter what it is.
—Thelma Elliott

Having a purpose, even a very simple purpose, is what keeps us going. It's important to acknowledge that doing great things isn't nearly as important as doing small things well. Making a few phone calls to some people we care about is one of the nicest of all small things. Running an errand for someone who can no longer drive is a huge gift with a mighty purpose, and one not soon forgotten. Even sharing an already-read newspaper with a neighbor who no longer is able to pay for one is a gigantic gift.

Too often we think the only purposes in life that count are the ones that impact a multitude of people. How wrong we are. Most of us will never do something that impacts thousands, but doing one tiny thing will bring happiness to one person, who will then pass on the gift in turn. In time, multitudes may indeed be impacted. But our focus is on one person, one act, one moment, one tiny difference that matters to at least two people: yourself and the one you have helped. That's reason enough to get out of bed every day.

We should never think we have no role to play in the lives of others. That they are present on our path means we do have a role. The size of the role is not important; what matters is just showing up.

9.

We see things not as they are, but as we are ourselves.
— H. M. Tomlinson

Projection is exceedingly powerful. Initially, we resist believing that what we see "out there" is our own creation — our own story. How can that be, we wonder. But in time, and with the willingness to believe that we do actually see what we want to see, everything about our lives can change — and for the better. Knowing that what lies before us is what we have created means that we can change the picture. Changing our minds — cultivating a more peaceful presence — will change what we see. Once we experience the power of this change in us, we will embrace the truth about the power of projection.

We can change who we are and how we will show up in our relationships. If we want to live softer lives, if we want to have kinder relationships, if we want to go to bed every night knowing we have lived a truly helpful day, the choice is always ours. What we send forth to others, who they see and thus who we see, rests solely with us.

What an exciting opportunity every moment is when we realize that how we are seen, as well as how we see, is solely tied to our intention.

10.

Wisdom lets us know that the key is not
to judge, but to love and nurture.
— Jane Nelson

Making the decision to forgo judging others isn't an easy, "do it once" decision. Most of us have to conscientiously monitor our thoughts because the inclination to sit in judgment of others calls to us with such regularity, sometimes even with intensity. But the choice to give up that defect is absolutely possible. Any habit can be broken, and that's what judging others has become. We must have a replacement, however; and there is no better one than to think a loving thought about every person who crosses our path or our mind.

This may seem like an impossible undertaking. Judging has become our very nature; however, expressing love can just as easily become our nature. We simply have to commit to it. We certainly have all crossed paths with people who seem to live in a constant state of kindness. They have nothing we don't have, except maybe a little willingness to show up in a more loving way. Let's give it a go. What do we have to lose?

Today is another fresh beginning. We can become whoever we choose to be today. Offering only love will change us as much as everyone else we encounter.

11.
So often we try to alter circumstances to suit ourselves, instead of letting them alter us.
—Mother Maribel

The need to control people and circumstances to suit us and our vision of how our journey should be often runs counter to God's vision for us. And then we are faced with a choice: Do we let go and let God run the show? Or do we dig in and live pretty miserable lives? Our willingness to let ourselves adjust to what is gives us significant peace of mind, and we can live in this space as a constant. It's nothing more than a simple decision; it's not always easy, perhaps, but it is simple.

Yet far too often, we stubbornly think we have a better plan. God lets us try it out too. We are not force-fed His vision. But if we are honest about how life is moving forward, the stumbling blocks we encounter give us reason to pause: Might there be a better way? Might not God have a better plan for each of us? Maybe it's time to rethink this journey. With God in charge, we will experience the right circumstances and reach the perfect destination at the right time. What could be easier than that?

Every day we are faced with one or more circumstances we feel compelled to change. Let's instead adjust to what is today and see how that feels. It's far less work and much less stressful too.

12.
Difficult periods might be opening the door to the perfect outcome we have been longing for.

We can't assume we know just why a situation has caught our attention, or perhaps even trapped us in its clutches. But we can learn from hindsight that what seemed baffling at the time was actually the perfect unraveling of a problem we didn't even know was on the horizon. We are always being led to the experiences we are meant to have. No experience that we must have to move us to the next level of understanding will be omitted. Each one will eventually come to us, and in time we will be grateful that it did.

God leaves nothing to chance. Occasionally, it may seem that He has taken a back seat, but He is always ready to help us get back on track. The door we need to walk through will open just as we approach it. In time, we will grow accustomed to the perfection of our lives. Everything has been well planned—everything.

We can look forward to each daybreak, knowing that God's presence will guide us all day long. If something feels especially difficult, move aside and let God walk in front.

13.
Asking God for help has finally become a part of my life. Now I'm learning to quiet myself to hear God's response.
—Joan Rohde

Being assured that God is ever present to guide, to comfort, and to love us unconditionally is all we really ever need to know. Yet too many of us continue to doubt on occasion. The good news is that God doesn't mind if we doubt. He won't abandon us regardless. He will never leave our side and doesn't actually mind if we fail to realize His presence. There is nothing codependent about God!

In most people's lives, every day a situation comes up where they wonder the best path to pursue. On far too many of these occasions, we let our ego decide which path is best. When ego has chosen, it's usually at the expense of someone else. The ego isn't ever guiding us to make the loving choice, but rather the selfish one, the one that serves only itself. God, on the other hand, helps us want what's best for all people.

Having a helpmate "on call" is a real gift, and that's exactly who God is in our lives. And He wants us to rely on Him continuously.

14.
There is no area of personal challenge in your life that God's love cannot solve.
—Mary Kupferle

The assurance of God's constant love every moment of our existence is the ultimate game changer. Many of us have lived with an uneasy reliance on God for much of our lives, but we can now give up this uneasiness. All we have to do is fully accept the truth of our lives instead. And the truth is that God has always been our constant companion. We didn't have to be consciously aware of it for it to be true. It's just so much nicer to know He is present. We can be at peace at last, if that's our choice.

How much easier it is to face a challenge of any size when we know we never have to face it alone. As a matter of fact, it's impossible to face it alone. We can block out God's guidance, of course; but we can't block out His presence. We can actually sail through life with ease when we remember that God is the captain of our boat. Be quiet and calmly go with the flow.

Today will be calm and fruitful in all the right ways if we embrace God and His love as the forever guiding force in our lives.

15.

Let us be willing to release old hurts.
—Martha Smock

Far too commonly, we tend to become obsessed with hanging
on to memories of past hurts. We have all done it, sometimes for
weeks, frequently for days at least. Why is it that we want to keep
punishing ourselves in this way? Nothing that has taken place need
hurt us for another second. In fact, most experiences we label as
hurtful were likely owing to our own perception. When we learn
that another person's treatment of us speaks volumes about them
and says nothing about us, we find relief.

Taking someone else's criticism as gospel gives them complete
power over who we are. Let's remember that we are in charge of
how we see others, how we hear others, and how we respond to
others. Let's not let others take charge of who we are and what
is clearly ours to control. Being hurt by anyone else can become
merely a bad dream. From now on, we need not be on the receiving
end of anyone's put-downs, whether intentional or accidental.

*Being free of the past, whatever it has held, is ours to celebrate. Today is a
new beginning.*

16.

The luxury of doing good surpasses every
other personal enjoyment.
—John Gay

What does it mean to "do good"? I suppose it depends on the doer.
But from my perspective, doing good means being considerate
of other people at all times. It means being kind at every turn. It
means showing up in a helpful way wherever we visit. And it means
truly listening to whomever is standing before us. Let's not forget,
they are on a mission that includes us.

Doing good feels good, both to the doer and the receiver. And the
more opportunities we take up for doing good, the greater will be
our contribution to the whole of society. Never forget, every good

act is paid forward. The more we are each responsible for taking good actions, the greater our impact is on our communities, our families, and the whole world. What we do for one, we are actually doing for all. Our reach is beyond what we can even imagine.

Today is a "do good" day. Actually, every day should be. And when we take this suggestion to heart, we will be assured of multiple good days too.

17.
Control is an illusion.
—Melodie Beattie

Our impulse to control other people and the myriad situations we are confronted with on a daily basis is extremely powerful, perhaps even addictive. What we find so very difficult to learn is that our desire to control always leads to frustration. Most often it leads to arguments that are unwinnable. Unless the other person relents and decides to do whatever it was we wanted, we are left disappointed or angry. And if they do change course, it's not because we have actually succeeded at controlling that other person. Most likely, they simply gave in.

What is it that makes us so intent on controlling others? I think it's fear. If others follow their own minds, they might choose to discard our friendship or worse. Rejection is anathema to us. If we can hang on tight to those people we think we need, we believe we'll be safe and that others will need us in return. How wrong our thinking is. Giving up control offers the joy we are actually seeking, but mostly we don't realize this, not until it's too late.

Every day is the perfect one to practice releasing control. It's an impossible task anyway. We can find joy only by letting fellow travelers be.

18.
So often I have tried to listen to everyone
else's truth and tried to make it mine.
— Liane Cordes

Parroting others' truths becomes habitual. It takes more than a little willingness to discern what we ourselves actually believe and why. Being unduly influenced by others' opinions happens so easily when one is searching for acceptance. Discovering what you alone believe necessitates sincere personal reflection. It also requires looking at one's past to see what situations occurred that were upsetting and then careful analysis to determine why. At our core, we do know what we believe. We just have to be daring enough to reveal it to ourselves.

Bombastic people surround us, and they can make it hard to stand up for our beliefs. But committing to our own understandings, and then implementing that commitment one situation at a time, is a beginning. We may perhaps be leery of this because the forcefulness of others can be very intimidating. But we don't ever have to argue with anyone. All we need to do is politely state our position and move on. Practice lessens the fear.

None of us wants to be intimidated. Knowing what our truth is, and then revealing it, is growth. Let's appreciate each opportunity to do this today.

19.
Wise sayings often fall on barren ground,
but a kind word is never thrown away.
— Arthur Helps

Kindness is the quickest avenue to peace of mind. Perhaps we don't realize how calming it can be to show kindness to friend and stranger alike. But if we try it a few times, we might be amazed. Reaching out a kind hand to someone else soon changes us. So it makes sense that we can stop any disruption to our sense of well-being in its tracks by offering the hand of kindness to someone else: any discouragement or angst, any fear or spark of anger, can be alchemically shifted. Our own mood is instantly transformed. Whomever we offer kindness to is likewise changed.

There really is no mystery to living a more peaceful life. Simple acts of kindness, random or intentional, will guarantee it. Why more of us don't practice these acts on a regular basis is no doubt owing to our self-absorption. We are always looking for what someone else might do for us. Let's be the "doers" instead. And watch how our lives change. This is in our control when not much else is.

Making the choice to toss kindness around like confetti is a wonderful gift to the world we are inhabiting. Experiment and see for yourself today.

20.
Listening means an unhurried time when God really can have a chance to imprint his thoughts in your mind.
—Frank N. D. Buchman

Meditation is often the avenue used to listen to God's messages. But carefully taking note of the words on the printed page that we haphazardly open to read at random, or finding the messages we seek in the words of a friend or even a stranger who has passed our way today, can also be God at work. What's always true is that God is trying to get our attention in myriad ways. Whether or not we are hearing the message depends entirely on our willingness to get out of our own way.

To know that God is always present in our minds is awesome, perhaps even startling to some. What it means is that we never have to search for God; He is here, now, always. Our only task is to be attentive, and that's a far bigger task some days than others. On days when we are troubled by someone else's behavior, or perhaps concerned about a health situation, it may seem as if God has moved. But on the contrary, that will never happen. There is not a lot in this life we can be absolutely rely on, but God's constant presence is one we can count on with certainty.

God is always waiting for us to turn a willing ear to His presence. He will always lead us to a peaceful moment, and the moments add up.

21.

**Life is made up of desires that seem big and vital
one minute, and little and absurd the next. I
guess we get what's best for us in the end.**
—Alice Caldwell Rice

Getting "what's best for us in the end" may not feel all that
comforting when it arrives. In time, however, deciding to be
grateful despite our first reaction does have a way of changing
how we perceive the experience. First reactions are often wrong,
primarily because we fail to see how the experience harmoniously
weaves itself into the panoply of experiences we have already had.
We do see, if we are willing to be objective about it, that all of our
life experiences have a rhythm about them that is quite perfect for
the part we are playing in the orchestra of life.

There are no mistakes to how our life is unfolding. Now, that
doesn't mean we can't misinterpret something that has happened,
but we will receive those lessons we were born to experience. We
can bypass them for a time, but, one by one, they will return, and
we will be the better for it. Getting what's best for us in the end is a
fact of our existence, and how lucky we are that this is so.

*There is far less mystery to our lives than we might have assumed. We are
generally the last to know what is headed our way, but it will be on time. And
God will be part of the process.*

22.

Find everyday reasons to dance.
—Elisabeth L.

When we think about dancing, most of us think about feeling joyful.
Finding reasons to be joyful every day is a great intention to set.
After all, we aren't here in this earthly classroom to be angry or
fearful. We are here to nurture those who are traveling by our sides.
We are here to serve as examples to those who are struggling with
a situation that we have already faced with success. And we are
here to simply be the holy presence of love in human form. In every

one of these instances, joy lies at the center—enough joy to freely dance about.

When we contemplate dancing, we think about being light-hearted, and that's a way to honor the God within us. We need not be filled with gloom and doom. There is nothing that will come our way to be handled today that can't be handled with the God within to guide us. In fact, the tougher the situation, the mightier the lesson. We can dance through every experience. We will be led. All we need to do is follow.

Today is reaching toward us in a gentle way. Let's enter expectantly and filled with awe. God has a hand in everything.

23.

Friendships bless us, teach us, guide us, and give us reason to pause, again and again. We need every one of them.

Having friends who really know us grounds us. And because so many experiences come to us daily that we didn't know were necessary to our learning curve, friends, coupled with God, help to settle us into a quiet place of acceptance. In fact, acceptance is the solution to every experience that pays a visit. We can't change what is destined to be part of the education we are meant to have. But we can gratefully accept it, knowing that it's perfect for us and that it's part of the patchwork needed for the completion of the quilt that is us.

We are becoming who we need to be with the help of our friends. God, too, is always playing His part. We don't really have a choice except for when we will surrender to the plan that is taking shape. It's nice knowing that who we are becoming is actually out of our hands in the final analysis. Our job is to stay centered and agree to the plan. It's quite perfect.

We can anticipate great opportunities today, opportunities to help others, opportunities to grow closer to who we are becoming, opportunities to better understand the presence of God in our lives.

24.

**Whether we are forty or sixty or eighty,
we are evolving right on schedule.**
— Sue Atchley

It's a comfort knowing that our lives are unfolding as intended.
Most of us didn't really appreciate this when we were younger.
More likely, we fretted over all the unexpected changes that were
happening, changes seemingly out of our control. Many of us are
only now realizing that God has always been a part of every change
that has come along. Never were we alone when a sudden shift
in our direction motioned to us, and we can count on that divine
presence, never changing in its constancy.

Learning that our life's pattern is by design doesn't take the joy out
of life, not at all. Not knowing what was coming didn't mean that
the experience was an unknown one. Indeed, whatever it was, it
came at the right time, in the perfect way, and in the company of
God. The understanding that our lives have been divinely scheduled
should alleviate some of the angst many of us feel. Just know that
we are always in partnership with God. All is under His control.

*Being at peace today is easy when we remember to remember that God is part
of everything that is on our schedule today.*

25.

It's all in the attitude.
— Eileen Fehlen

These five simple words carry truth as few others do. Our attitudes
do indeed color everything we see and experience. Even an
extremely dire situation can be handled with equanimity if our
attitude is one of hope and trust. Of course, what must precede the
good attitude is willingness to remember how very present God is
in every experience. Because we forget about His presence, we too
often become fearful, and that can lead to conflict where none was
called for, initiated by an unhappy and generally scared ego.

Fortunately, we can nurture a good attitude. Perhaps the easiest way to do that is to do a daily gratitude list. This is not a new suggestion. We have no doubt received this advice from a friend in the past, perhaps one who has noticed how negatively we have responded to a circumstance in our life. The power to change how we see the world around us by making a gratitude list is awesome. It's as though we have flipped on a light switch in a very dark room. Reflecting on all we have to be grateful for is a sure way to heal a bad attitude. If in doubt, try it sometime soon.

Doing a gratitude list can change our entire worldview. It's a power that can't be overestimated. Today just may be the day for you to write one. Don't tarry.

26.

There are two entirely opposite attitudes possible in facing the problems of one's life. One, to try and change the external world; the other, to try and change oneself.
— Joanna Field

It is so difficult to accept that the external world is simply not something we can control. The itch to try is so powerful, but we are foiled at every attempt. Now, something may change in a way that pleases us on its own, but if it does, it's not because of anything we did. We need to understand that. Actually, we need to be grateful for that. The burden we'd be saddled with if the entire world outside us was ours to control would wear us down very quickly.

On the other hand, we do have absolute power to change ourselves in a nanosecond. We may still have to dedicate ourselves to making a habit of the change we are committed to; old behaviors don't die easily. But it's thrilling to realize that any change we want to make in our behavior is immediately on our radar screen. Making these changes is as doable as our willingness permits.

Today may offer us an opportunity to change ourselves in a way that will be significant over time. Be on the lookout. We will recognize when making a change will make a difference.

27.

Loving others is easier if I keep it simple.

Loving others isn't always as easy as it sounds. Changing others to our liking, which we think will make them easier to love, isn't an option. We either make the decision to love others or we don't. It's a black or white issue. There's no in-between. If we come to believe that "all those others" are our teachers on this pathway of learning, we can adjust how we see them. They are present to stretch us, to educate us, and to ease our strong desire to control those who aren't ours to control.

Beginning each day with the intention of loving everyone the way we love the God of our understanding eases our journey. It's easier to set the intention, of course, than to live it. But practice can change us. And the truth is, everyone deserves our love. Everyone is a child of God, as are you and I. We need each other in order to become who we have been created to be. And that means we need those who sometimes seem difficult to love as much as we need the small child we adore.

Everything in our lives is easier if we keep it simple. Loving others is just one of those things.

28.

Practiced consistently, new habits become who I am.
— Lin Andrukat

Most of us reading this have at least one bad habit that we find unworthy. And all too often, it's a habit that just keeps hounding us. There is only one way to escape a bad habit, and that's by developing a good one and then willingly practicing it consistently. Setting the intention upon arising that the good habit will be front and center all day long in our encounters with others is what it takes — nothing less.

Does this sound difficult? Perhaps. But we are very practiced at bad old habits. And they became habits because we defaulted to that behavior again and again. There is no new twist here, only a new choice. Perhaps the easiest decision is this: affirm "I will act from a peaceful heart all day today." And then grade yourself. Feel good about every encounter where you remained peaceful. Forgive yourself for every time you failed, affirming your intention to do better the next time.

Changing a bad habit isn't that difficult if we make the new habit a simple one. Try being peaceful.

29.
We are living in a world that is absolutely transparent, and God is shining through it all the time.
— Thomas Merton

Aren't we a lucky group of men and women? We have a very present God and the constancy of a peaceful mind if we so choose. I think as we age, the desire for a more peaceful mindset increases, at least, that's been my experience. Agitation tires us out. Even worse, it invites unnecessary judgment of others. If we believe that God is shining through everything all of the time, we'll never feel the call to judge or worse. We will instead be on the lookout for opportunities to toss love around indiscriminately.

There is no better time than right now to choose a new approach to how we perceive every person and every experience that grabs our attention as well. In every instance, what we see is meant for our eyes in that moment. The power of the truth of this is awesome. God is shining through everything. There can simply be no other way, now or ever.

What my day looks like is entirely up to me. God is present to show me the perfect day if I let Him.

30.

**Turn a disadvantage into an advantage;
embrace that which is unfair.**
— Eileen Fehlen

The truth of the matter is that everything is advantageous when
we consider the long view of our lives. Some experience that we
were so certain was awful actually opened the door to make us fully
ready for the very next growth spurt in our existence. Admittedly,
it's not always easy to remember this when the calamity occurs.
That's why hindsight is so crucial to our understanding of where
we have been and where we might be going next. There truly
are no wrong turns on our journey, only detours that we don't
yet understand.

When we finally embrace the reality that God is present and has
always been present, we will walk toward the next unknown with
a quieter mind and a more peaceful heart. With God, nothing
is askew — nothing. When at first glance life looks unfair, it just
hasn't yet been looked at with the eyes of God. We have heard it
many times, but one more time is perhaps required: *all is well* — now
and always.

*We have the power to determine how we see any experience that we will have
today. Will we choose to see it as advantageous? With God's help, we can.*

OCTOBER

1.

Whoever is happy will make others happy too.
—Anne Frank

I do think happiness is a choice, as clearly a choice as peace of mind, the expression of love, and kindness to friend and stranger alike. But the opposite of all of these choices is available to each of us as well. Which choice we make is as personal as what shirt or dress we put on for a special occasion or how we answer the door or the phone when someone is reaching out to us. How we live each moment tells others who we are. Our actions speak even louder than words. Do we offer a smile accompanying the hand with which we reach out to a stranger?

Happiness is contagious, I think, and there are so many ways to spread a bit of happiness around. How we greet anyone, whether at the store, the front door, or the dinner table, is a sure sign of our mood. When our emotional state is a happy one, we can observe how it initiates a kind response from others. The best part about being happy is that it allows us to live stress-free lives. The power of choice can't be overestimated.

Happiness is a byproduct of our choices today. To choose it moment by moment becomes a habit that can benefit the whole world.

2.

To keep a lamp burning, we have to keep putting oil in it.
—Mother Teresa

We can't rest on our laurels; we must keep actively living more loving and peaceful lives if we want to make a difference that will change the world for the better. And we do that by being vigilant about how we respond to all the people we encounter throughout the day. We can't just be occasionally kind and loving. We can't be choosy about who we think deserves our kindness. Our interactions need to be consistently loving—the kind of interaction that would make God happy.

Is this a hard decision to make? I think not. Some would say it's really far simpler to know how we are always going to show up, rather than taking each encounter under advisement before responding. Learning once and for all to be our better selves is the fast track to consistently peaceful lives. And isn't that what we are all seeking, after all? Isn't that what God wants for all of us as well?

Daily vigilance about how our actions affect others is far better than living willy-nilly, and making the choice to add benefit wherever we go eliminates the guesswork.

3.
God allows us to experience the low points of life in order to teach us lessons we could not learn in any other way.
—C. S. Lewis

When we allow ourselves to look at our lives from this perspective instead of simply being angry about life's tough lessons, we will more graciously become the people we were born to be. Each one of us came into this world with a set of lessons to master. And some spiritual teachers say that we each actually agreed to our individual lessons before we arrived in our current incarnation via birth. That idea may be a reach for some of us, but what is more easily accepted is that we do hit challenges along the path and that they do push us to stretch in new and important ways.

But whether we find ourselves on an upward trajectory or in a valley of despair, we should always keep in mind that we haven't been forgotten. We are always in the presence of God, who is always waiting for our call for help. There is no challenge too big for us to handle if we rely on the ready hand of God.

Let no challenge go unmet today. Each one is coming to us perfectly, and the sole and sufficient help we need to manage it is merely a prayer away.

4.

If you think you are too small to make a difference, try sleeping with a mosquito.
—Dalai Lama

Although this quote by the Dalai Lama may make us smile, there is great wisdom within it. Each one of us can make a difference in the lives of everyone we touch, and it doesn't take a very big effort, either. Something as small as a smile can make a difference. Taking the time to listen to someone who needs to talk can be a turning point for them. And what's equally important is that every small, kind thing we do makes a difference in our lives too.

What can be hard to remember is that every action any of us takes is felt far and wide. Think for a moment about the butterfly effect. Cause and effect constantly hold sway over even the tiniest of gestures, as research scientists are learning. So think again if you discount the importance of your impact on the greater whole every time you choose to be kind or to offer the hand of peace in the moment.

Even though we are powerless over the actions of others, we are in control of ourselves, and we can make a difference today with someone, somewhere.

5.

You could not remove a single grain of sand from its place without thereby changing something throughout all parts of the immeasurable whole.
—Fichte, *The Vocation of Man*

The Gaia Theory (a.k.a. the Gaia Hypothesis) as expressed in this quotation, explains the connectedness between all of humanity as well as other living beings. We are not separate from one another, not at all. Let's not misunderstand what's undeniably true. What any one of us does is felt elsewhere too. And if we doubt this, we are prone to dismiss the constant impact our actions are having on others every moment—a grave mistake to be sure.

To be fully connected to one another is a very good thing, and it's a really good thing to understand and honor this idea. It simply means that what we do to one, we are doing to everyone. And if we want to have a positive impact on those we love, we will also be making a positive impact even on all those we don't even know. Nothing pleases God more than this. It's not about doing great things, but doing tiny things well, as Mother Teresa so famously said.

It simplifies our lives to know that all we need to do is concern ourselves with what we do in the moment. Making that tiny action gentle and kind is quite enough.

6.

Doubt is a pain too lonely to know that faith is his twin brother.
— Kahlil Gibran

It seems that it is much easier to be ruled by doubt than faith. Why is this? I think there's a simple reason, actually. We all have default beliefs, and when we are confronted by a situation whose outcome has us worried, we far too often easily slide into being doubtful that the outcome will be to our liking. What we fail to remember is that the outcome is in God's hands, so we can be free of worry and doubt and simply rest with the outcome that is best for all concerned if we choose to do so. And of course, that just happens to be the most peaceful choice too.

Because of our too-easy tendency to slide into doubt, we make our lives far more stressful than they need be. God is in charge. Period! The sooner we appreciate that fact, the easier our lives will become. We all deserve greater peace of mind, regardless of how old or young we are, and the choice to claim it stands before us always. All we need to do is surrender to the easier, softer way.

Consciously choosing to trust God today is an intention we can make. It is by far the decision that will give us the most peace.

7.

Sometimes the things that frighten you the most can be the biggest sources of strength.
—Iris Timberlake

Most of us learn as we mature that strength is always ours if we turn to a Higher Power for help during the times that feel most daunting. Alone, we generally don't have the strength to handle the crises that can upend our lives. And we can't really be expected to have all the answers we need or the wisdom to handle challenges that have never before shown up on our radar. But God has spoken and said, "I am here. Rely on me." And when we do, we have all the strength we need, as well as perfect solutions for whatever troubles us.

Being reminded that we will never be given more than we—along with God—can handle is such a comfort. Truer words were never uttered. What's also true is that far too often, we don't remember to rely on God for His part. We think we must handle whatever stands before us alone, and we falter, assuming we are failures rather than realizing we have simply forgotten the most important part of the equation: God.

With God's help we will never lack strength or wisdom. Today is a good day to apply this principle.

8.

If I had to describe something as divine, it would be what happens between people when they really get it together.
—June L. Tapp

What Tapp is describing is the holy instant, I think. It is in that moment, or collection of moments, that there is no sense of separation between two people. When minds join for a greater purpose with the full attention of everyone involved, it is a divine time indeed. Not every gathering leads to people getting completely on the same wavelength. But when people are called together by a Higher Presence, both their feelings and subsequent activities are elevated.

Appreciating those truly divine moments is one way to invite more of them. We have to be open to the next moment and whatever it brings with it if we want to honor the precious life we have been given. Remember, there is only one you. And never forget that the coming together of all of us into the Divine One that is God is our true reality. Being aware of our part in this Wholeness can not only change our perspective, it will always provide the well-being we crave.

Taking care to be fully present to everyone today will provide us with many holy instants. Such moments feel good because they move us into the loving arms of God.

9.
What if we knew what lay ahead?

How many times a day do you hear yourself or someone with you say, "If only I had known." We mistakenly think that life would be so much easier if we knew exactly what lay ahead. However, I think that if we knew, we'd feel much greater anxiety. A far better way to look at the future is to trust that what is going to happen *is known*, just not by us at this time. And we have been fully prepared for our future by all our experiences that have preceded it.

As has been said many times in many places, we don't ever need to worry about how our lives will unfold. There is a perfect plan at work and a perfect orchestrator. Our assignment is to play our part to the best of our ability; God will see to all of the rest. Because this is the truth of how life is unfolding, it's really just as good as knowing exactly what lies ahead. God is our companion as we wander forth. Need I say more?

What is on our agenda today is perfect for this point in our journey. That we know and can celebrate.

10.
Retreat is not defeat.
— Kay Lovatt

Retreating from a potential conflict might be a smart choice. So is retreating from a noisy group when we are in need of quiet meditation and prayer. Let's not misunderstand: retreating doesn't mean we are uninterested. It often simply means we need time alone to think more clearly about the options that are on the table. Retreating can also be another word for detachment. Detaching from others who are on the attack, either against us or those we care about, is taking an obvious stand, though a quiet one.

As is evident, there are myriad ways of interpreting the act of retreating, and not one of them means the person who opts to retreat has been defeated. The decision to take better care of oneself is the most obvious explanation for retreating. Any time we can step away from a situation that's gone sideways, we will have added measurable benefit to the world we share with so many others.

We can always look the other way when an invitation to conflict is headed our way. In this situation, retreat is a wise move. No one gets hurt.

11.
Situations can look very bad one day and more manageable the next. The only thing that has changed is my perspective.
— Sandy Lamberson

Our perspective holds the key to how we see everything before us. Some believe that what our perspective reflects back to us is whatever we are projecting outward. That might not seem plausible, but careful monitoring of our thoughts will generally confirm it. However, even understanding this truth doesn't relieve us of the need to be responsible for how we react to all the opportunities destined to be ours. And never forget that what appears to be a bad situation might actually be opening the door to the greatest opportunity we have ever experienced.

We sit in the seat of power. Our attitude is the turning point for how our life is unfolding. And no one can control it but us. We can decide to restart any day if we have awakened snarly or unsure of ourselves. Generally, when we are plagued by a bad attitude, it's because we have forgotten to count our blessings. Making a gratitude list each morning, even a very short one, can turn the day around. Doing this every day can turn one's life around.

It's far easier to be happy than you might think. Begin by gently thanking all the people you care about. They are not crossing your mind accidentally.

12.
Hesitation just might be the easiest pathway to a peaceful day.

The power in hesitation is palpable. Responding too quickly to any situation can be unwise. But when something has provoked anger, pausing even for a few moments allows for a changed perspective; within those few moments, we can perceive a truth that may have initially failed to get our attention.

Perhaps it's hard to accept that simply saying or doing nothing when our ire has been triggered is the best response. But making the decision to give this idea a try is the best way to discover the wisdom inherent in it. We will instantly feel a sense of relief when we turn away from conflict. Not adding injury where none is called for is listening to the inner voice of God. We may not even realize we are making a profound decision when we choose to let a situation slide by us rather than responding in kind to someone else's anger, but indeed, that's the power of the quiet pause. Practicing it, one experience at a time, changes us profoundly.

Today will quite likely offer us at least one opportunity to pause rather than mindlessly respond to a situation best left alone. What fun to put this idea into practice.

13.

**The worst sin toward our fellow creatures is not
to hate them, but to be indifferent to them.**
— George Bernard Shaw

Apathy toward those we pass on the street, at the grocery, or
wherever we cross paths is so diminishing. It has been said that
the kindest gift we can offer another human being is rapt attention.
And we need not know the people we may be encountering to take
notice of them. Letting any person we encounter know that he or
she isn't invisible to us is a way of honoring them. We all deserve to
have our humanity recognized.

Many of us grew up in families where we felt invisible or perhaps
just the opposite: constantly in the spotlight. Either response from
others fails to see us for who we really are: thinking, breathing,
feeling human beings. Showing others they have been noticed by
us is the most holy of all encounters. There is no magic to setting an
intention for doing this today. It's really a simple decision.

*Our indifference toward others actually reflects how we feel about ourselves.
Perhaps this is a good day to take notice and make an inventory of the kind of
person we are inside.*

14.

**Do your little bit of good where you are; it's those little
bits of good put together that overwhelm the world.**
— Desmond Tutu

Making the intention, every day, to do just a little bit of good feels
so manageable. Nary a one of us can fail at a task as simple as this
one. A little bit of good comes in all sizes and shapes. It might be
calling a friend you haven't spoken to for a while. Or it might be
stopping by a neighbor's house to see if there is something you can
pick up for her when you go to the store. Or it can be even easier,
just smiling at the first stranger you see standing on the corner.

God expects so little of each one of us; however, for the world to
be overwhelmed by goodness, we all have to participate. The good

news is that participating in making the world better by committing to a simple daily act of kindness also has a huge impact on us as the person taking the action. What we do for others blesses us tenfold. Let's not duck doing what's right today. So many will profit, not least of whom will be ourselves.

We are always in the right place to do the next right thing. Making it an act of goodness is life-changing for us as well as others.

15.

Never believe that a few caring people can't change the world. For, indeed, that's all who ever have.
—Margaret Mead

Most people have at some time lamented that the world is in need of change. There are those who worry about climate change, and with good reason. Multitudes worry about the numbers of people who are food insecure, in this country as well as around the world. And racial unrest and injustices are crying for attention too. Many feel called to respond.

The good news is that each one of us can have an impact in at least a small way on any crisis that calls out to us. It's not about orchestrating a huge response but doing one tiny thing that lies before us. Making the choice to be a caring person, one day at a time, is not a huge commitment. But if that feels like too much, break the day down into smaller increments. Consider doing one loving thing every morning for a week and see how different your life feels.

Doing even a tiny kindness will reverberate, eventually touching a person on the other side of the world. Does that seem impossible? Think again.

16.

Anger dwells only in the bosom of fools.
—Albert Einstein

How often in a week, or even a day, do we lose ourselves in a few minutes of anger? Fear is generally the underlying factor, and it wears many masks. For certain it impedes our well-being, but it also interferes with the journey we are making—a journey that includes everyone else on the path of being. Anger separates people, and our purpose in this life is to join with all those whom God has selected to travel this road of life with us.

Anger can actually be interpreted as an opening to a deeper discussion with someone. The anger is undoubtedly covering something up, generally something in ourselves that we are trying to deny and externalize, but if we use it as an opportunity to have a deeper talk, it can make a huge positive difference. And that reintegration isn't limited to just the two who have the conversation but touches everyone either person encounters throughout the rest of the day as well. Opening our hearts to any other individual has the capacity to transform our dialogue with everyone.

Today can be a game changer. Greet anger over anything as an opportunity for closeness, not separation.

17.

In a world where there is so much to be done, I felt strongly impressed that there must be something for me to do.
—Dorothea Dix

Nothing has really changed since Dix made this statement in the mid-nineteenth century. There is still much to be done. Her devotion to caring for the mentally ill, though specific in its focus, can be seen as a model for caring for all people in general. The work she did was about treating people humanely, a model of reform that each one of us can adopt in our own lives. We don't need to be focused on any specific group of people, but rather focused with kindness on one person at a time.

There is nothing complicated about making the choice to incorporate a fresh perspective on the people we are destined to encounter on our journey. As I've said myriad times, no one is heading our way accidentally. Each person is seeking our specific personal attention. Can we offer it nonjudgmentally? We may not feel great love for everyone, but accepting that he or she has come to participate in a lesson each of us is destined to receive is all that's asked of us. All we need to do is agree.

There is much to be done today. But let's begin small. Choose kindness in every encounter.

18.

Enveloping ourselves in each moment as it comes eases every step of the journey, each and every day.

We are so commonly called to the past through a memory that is triggered, most often by a present circumstance. Rather than staying in the present, we may wander through the corridors of the past, far too often living there while missing the only time that actually counts: this moment. Relishing *now* can be habit-forming if we are attentive. Our vigilance is what makes the difference.

Vacillating between depression and anxiety defines life for many of us. But both conditions can be relieved quite quickly if we soak up the rhythms of this moment alone. They do call to us (in fact, we can feel them) but our minds remain far too undisciplined. Fortunately, this is a condition that we can address with just a tiny bit of willingness. Living in the past is seldom very satisfying, and dwelling on what may come in the future is unsettling for the most part. The only place we can simply *be* is here and now. Why not choose it?

Be here now. Breathe in this moment —and no other.

19.

Being happy doesn't mean that everything is perfect. It means that you have decided to look beyond the imperfections.

Perfection is beyond reach. Not even God is looking for perfection from us. Doing the best we can in whatever we are taking on is definitely good enough. We often expect perfection from ourselves and from one another too, but none of us really knows what perfection even looks like. We do know what trying one's best looks like, however. We can observe that in ourselves and one another every day.

When we come to understand that doing our best is really good enough, we can be at peace and finally know happiness. It's so much easier to live day by day when we set more reasonable goals for ourselves. Looking beyond our own imperfections, and others' as well, is the *"perfect"* goal. And joy soon overcomes us as we do this.

Happiness is clearly a choice, one that can be made within every encounter. What a simple way to live at long last.

20.
Don't think too much. You'll create a problem that wasn't even there in the first place.

This quote may well make us smile; hopefully, we also realize it has more than a grain of truth to it. We so easily complicate our lives by imagining problems that have no substance. Of course, that's because we fail to stay in the present moment. In the here and now, we can be quite sure that all is well. There is nary a problem when we keep our mind focused on this moment and the power of the presence of God, however we define Him.

Isn't it an interesting realization that we truly are problem free? Any wrinkle in our perception is always because we have taken our focus off of God and this sacred moment. The ego part of our mind never wants us to feel free of problems, nor does it want us to put our attention on God. The ego sees God as the enemy. *A Course in Miracles* tells us that we have two voices in our mind. One of them is the voice of the ego, which speaks first and loudest and is always wrong. However, there is another voice. Let's listen to it and know peace.

Today will offer us the opportunity to choose the voice we want as our guide. Let's choose carefully.

21.
What others think of you is none of your business.

How well I remember when I first heard this quote. In all honesty, it mystified me. I had spent decades imagining what others thought of me and then trying to either live up to their beliefs or change them. My focus was always "out there." As I gained maturity and an inkling of wisdom, I realized I couldn't change what others thought. But I could change myself, and if I was pleased with how I was showing up within the relationships that truly mattered to me, as well as with people I'd never even met before, I could be content.

The truth is that while we can't ever change another person's assessment of us, we can always change how we interact with each person we meet. Coming to terms with this verity means we constantly have opportunities to put our best foot forward. And then if people think well of us, great. If not, we will still feel good about who we were in the encounter. Their dismissal of us speaks volumes about them.

How others assess us today derives from their own self-assessment. Who they see is who they are. This is true of us as well.

22.

There is nothing the body suffers the soul may not profit by.
— George Meredith

We are not always eager to believe a statement like Meredith's. And yet, when we do, we realize how much more positive we feel about each experience we are having. There is good that comes from everything. And when we allow our minds to embrace this idea, we will see how much easier it is to walk through every occurrence that motions to us on a daily basis.

Our souls are always expanding and our hearts grow more open every time we willingly accept a situation, even one that we initially resisted. And just maybe, those we did resist, open our hearts even more than the ordinary situations. That our hearts open, just as our souls expand, is owing to our willingness to see the good in every experience that has beckoned. We will always be called by those experiences that we specifically need to fulfill the purpose for which we have been born. This we know absolutely.

Eagerly anticipating the experiences that have been selected for our growth today makes each one of them far more meaningful. Not one of them visits by mistake.

23.
Don't take life too seriously. We were put here to laugh.
— Helen Casey

Looking at life from a sunnier perspective also encourages us to initiate laughter in others. But of course, not everything that happens in life is laughable. Tragedies happen in families, communities are torn asunder by brutalities involving one group pitted against another, and nations are at war throughout the world. However, finding at least one thing every day that we can smile about is the very balm we need to eventually heal the entire planet. It won't happen overnight, but every instance of laughter moves us closer to a global community of smiling inhabitants.

Being willing to cultivate a lighter perspective on the daily happenings in our lives changes us profoundly. Doing so doesn't mean we don't empathize with the folks who are hurting because of circumstances beyond their control. Nor does it mean that we turn away rather than offering a helping hand when someone close by needs our compassionate response. Remember, anyone who crosses our path is there by appointment. But we can be that helper while wearing a hopeful smile just as easily as wearing a look of defeat.

We don't know just what today may offer us. But we can be pretty certain that being light-hearted will make the circumstances more manageable, whatever they may be.

24.
One of the most difficult things is not to change society — but to change yourself.
— Nelson Mandela

Why is it that changing ourselves is so difficult? There are probably a host of reasons, but the one that seems the most obvious is that we are responding in a habitual way to the experiences we encounter.

To change even one single habit takes awareness of ourselves, the willingness to choose an alternative behavior, and then commitment. None of us change any habit overnight; they are deeply ingrained. However, we can make the decision to change any one of them in a nanosecond.

Let's begin by being willing to take a careful inventory of who we have become, both the good and the bad traits. This takes humility coupled with courage, along with willingness. In fact, the willingness must come first. The good news is that we can change. Maybe the worst trait we have will take significant effort to shift, but the place to begin is by choosing a small one to begin with so that we get the feel of what it takes to succeed in transforming a long-held pattern. We will become who we'd rather be, in time.

Is today the day to look more carefully at who we are? Is there something about ourselves we need to change? This task is not too large to achieve. Remember, God is our guide.

25.

**It takes a rare person to want to hear
what he doesn't want to hear.
— Dick Cavett**

We surely don't always want to hear what's ultimately good for us. But each essential message will keep presenting itself, first from one voice and then from another, until we finally surrender to it. There are lessons we have agreed to experience on this journey, and they will not let us alone until we take them in and make them part of our awareness.

Perhaps this sounds farfetched to you. But my eight decades of living have introduced me to myriad ideas that I initially discounted. One of those truths is the belief that our experiences are quite particular to who we are being individually guided to become. I now love resting in the knowledge of this, because it takes the worry about what might be coming next and lays it aside. Each successive realization on the agenda for each of us to know is part of the beautiful tapestry that is our life. Each thread is a necessary experience, one that contributes to the perfect picture that is us.

Growing accustomed to the idea that we will hear what we need to hear can give us great relief. All is well and is happening as it should.

26.
Advice from others applies to them.
—Georgette Vickstrom

How true. Yet so many are eager to try and convince us that their advice is just what we need. And when they are unable to let go of their need to give us advice, it all too often leads to disharmony. Sharing our experience, strength, and hope is one thing. Giving advice that's not requested is something far different. Keep in mind that we can never see what another person is experiencing except through our own lens, which of course means we aren't really seeing it at all. We are seeing our own story.

It's not wrong to want to be helpful; in fact, it's generally an indication of kindness. But gently offering a suggestion is far different from giving unasked-for advice. However, the best approach is always to inquire if our friend is interested in hearing our perspective. If the answer is no, honor that. It's not a put-down. It's simply allowing our friend to choose her own path.

Taking note of everyone who travels alongside us is what God wants from us each day. Being aware and attentive is our greatest gift to others.

27.
Being responsible for ourselves is a task
large enough for each of us.

The belief that we need to take on Herculean tasks in order to count in this life is what gets many of us off track. Keep in mind that we have been told by any number of spiritual giants that it's not about *how much we do*, but rather *how we do* whatever we are called to do. All we are ever expected to do to fulfill God's expectations is to be a responsible human being who interacts in a kind way; in fact, that's what we were born to do.

Many of us easily get trapped into thinking we need to do for others what they clearly need to do for themselves. This might be because we have surrounded ourselves with people who have lived irresponsibly and we felt compelled to pick up the slack to save them from the consequences of their behavior. While our intentions may have felt right, doing for others what they need to do for themselves shortchanges them of their own journey. None of us can become who God needs us to be by just sliding by.

What today offers us is the next right thing for each of us. Each one of us gets what is needed. Let's allow each other individual to handle what is clearly theirs.

28.
We may have all come on different ships, but we're in the same boat now.
—Martin Luther King Jr.

Amen. And the boat we share is often in turbulent water. But we can contribute to smooth sailing if we choose to see the best in one another in every moment. That doesn't mean others are always acting from a place of love—on the contrary. Others may be contributing to major havoc and disharmony, but their actions need not ever determine our responses. It's truly amazing for us when we at last become fully aware that what others do never needs to control what we choose to do.

Because we are all "on the same boat," so to speak, it's crucial that we embrace this new awareness. It will save us from more of the same heartache that has troubled us for so many years. Others share our journey for a reason; that's true, but it's never to control who we choose to be in any instance. We can always decide to be the one on the metaphoric boat who encourages a smooth voyage.

We can look to this day with joyful anticipation. It will usher in the perfect set of circumstances, and we will know just what to do.

29.

Nobody told me how hard and lonely change is.
—Joan Gilbertson

Change is a constant in our lives. There are periods when we take it in stride. However, we all face changes we'd rather not have to deal with, and they so often come at unexpected times. But is that really true? Some spiritual teachers have said that no unintended change will ever visit us and that the timing of each one will always be perfect. We may not feel ready for life's transformations, but we have actually been prepared for them. We simply didn't recognize the preparation when we were going through it.

The upside of this idea is that change means we are moving forward. The problem is we don't know what the destination is. That's where trust comes in; we can trust that God is part of every change we are called to make. In fact, it's God's plan for our lives that any change that calls to us is His will. Our peace is enhanced if we trust each change that beckons. God will never lead us astray. We never experience any change without His presence. We can relax in the knowledge that this is the truth.

Today may include a call to move in a new direction. If so, remember God is the source of this inspiration. Walk forward confidently.

30.

What a strange pattern the shuttle of life can weave.
—Frances Marian

And nearly eight billion patterns have been woven to date. A fascinating ancillary consideration is that no two human patterns are alike. We have similar threads, of course, but the final design we are moving toward is unique to our specific life events, experiences that were meant only for us and in a particular order. That's an amazing truth when we slow down long enough to ponder it. And we manage to intersect with the patterns of one another at the perfect moment as well. No meeting is a chance encounter! Our lives have been perfectly orchestrated.

Hopefully, that thrills you. I'm also hopeful that it gives you complete trust in the journey you have been invited to make. It's not haphazard; it's been designed with you in mind, you and all the other individuals you will meet or have already met. When we breathe in the depth of this truth, we are changed in the right way. We know, without a shadow of a doubt, that God has been part of the journey.

Today will be "just what the Doctor ordered." Walking into every experience expecting goodness will ensure it.

31.
It is the heart which experiences God and not the reason.
— Blaise Pascal

The experience of God can be constant and eternal. He simply never leaves our side. In fact, He resides within us. Now, this doesn't mean that as we live we are always conscious of His presence, but He is there — or rather, *here* — regardless. Personally, I so appreciate the idea that God doesn't need me to be aware of Him for Him to stick around.

When we factor this into our everyday experiences, it makes each one of them so much easier to handle. No experience ever catches up with us without our protector on board, and knowing that makes for smooth sailing. Now of course we may fall into periods of doubt, forgetting that God is our constant companion. But either way, God always sticks around — for everything.

Each day offers another opportunity to remember that God is with us for everything that comes to pass. His constant presence eliminates any uncertainty about how each new day will be.

NOVEMBER

1.

It is important to expect nothing, to take every experience, including the negative ones, as merely steps on the path, and to proceed.
— Ram Dass

It's not all that easy to expect nothing. Many of us are driven by our expectations of ourselves and especially others, but we can choose to form a new way to look at the collection of companions around us. For instance, we can decide that they are doing what seems like the best option for them, and then we can detach from it, knowing that what they have chosen doesn't have to impact us at all. We are always in charge of how we see and then interpret the actions of others.

We are all steadily proceeding on our own particular life's journey, and we encounter one another at the perfect intersections. That doesn't mean, however, that we will always like what we observe. Each experience will be something we can learn from though, and that's a key understanding we can celebrate. Our destination is made clearer with each encounter.

Who we see today has not come our way by accident. Look carefully and appreciate the lessons offered.

2.

When someone shows you who they are, believe them the first time.
— Maya Angelou

Our personal impact on others cannot be overestimated. Making a friend, or even a total stranger, feel like she or he matters to you in a particular encounter is the kindest of all gifts that we can bestow. Far too many of us go through life feeling we don't really matter to others — that our presence isn't even noted, a feeling of inestimable sadness.

We will never love (or even like) every experience we have with each of the people we encounter. But the point of every interaction is to give each one of us the opportunity to make the other person feel seen, feel heard, and feel appreciated simply for their presence. We can never pay too much attention to our fellow travelers. Those who cross our paths need to know they matter. Let's not be selfish with our attention.

Today will surely offer us multiple opportunities to pay loving attention to someone near us. Don't let them pass.

3.
Sometimes I'm awfully impressed by fools.
—Kelly Q.

How we respond in that moment of connection with other individuals who cross our path says a lot about who we are. Being open to how everyone presents himself is gracious and certainly is what's most pleasing to the God of our understanding. We truly don't know the backstory of everyone we meet. Behavior that seems ludicrous to us may, in fact, fit the situations that this stranger on our path commonly encounters. We can't know in detail why each person does what she does, but we can accept them where they are. Even better, we need to affirm them where they are. Anything less than that shortchanges all of us.

Being attentive to the people who are making up our story is of paramount importance. In fact, it is never accidental when others appear in our life, but that doesn't mean our connection will always be a pleasant one. Many of our teaching moments feel uncomfortable, but hindsight always reveals how those experiences fit into the bigger story of our lives. We all have a bigger story; in fact, every single experience is a paragraph, or perhaps even a chapter, in the story of who we are becoming.

Our stories are being written today. Let's pay attention and move with the story line.

EACH DAY A RENEWED BEGINNING

Every moment wasted looking back
keeps us from moving forward.
— Hillary Clinton

I don't want to suggest we shouldn't review our lives. In fact, reviewing how we did at the end of the day can help us to chart a better day tomorrow. But letting the past absorb us so completely that we miss out on what's coming our way is a serious mistake. We can only live one moment at a time; to waste any of them means not really inhabiting the present time.

We are so blessed to have a blueprint for moving through life, and we can decide to follow it. Breathe in one moment at a time; see each fellow traveler fully; deeply listen to his or her message, whatever it is; and let it add color to the picture your life is painting. Completely accepting everything that shows up to be part of our lives means we are attuned to the message God has devised specifically for us. Remember that if we look to the past too much we will not be able to learn life's lessons.

How exciting to know that God is the senior teacher and that all the people we encounter are on assignment in ways He has orchestrated. Let's not overlook anyone.

5.

To handle yourself, use your head; to
handle others, use your heart.
— Eleanor Roosevelt

We all certainly recognize when other fail to use their heads. But do we always recognize it when we ourselves do the same? How often are we guilty of acting thoughtlessly, providing ample evidence of not using either our heads or our hearts? Being conscious of how we are coming across to others in conversations relies on our awareness of both our heads and our hearts. It might even be said that we don't ever honestly communicate with anyone without relying on both.

There are certain tests we can apply to better understand how we are presenting ourselves to others. First, are we taking into account how they will hear what we are about to say? Pausing before saying anything is a great technique; during the pause, ask yourself, "Is what I am about to say or do going to please God?" If we find that question makes us hesitate for even a minute, it is likely whatever we were going to say or do is best passed over. Leading from our hearts in all matters gets much easier with practice.

Today will be a true test of our willingness to pause to consider how others might hear our comments. We don't have to say everything that comes into our minds.

6.

Another's opinion doesn't define anything about me. Only my actions do that.

I have heard it said that what other people think of us is none of our business. But I spent most of my life early on allowing anyone's opinion of me (or what I assumed was their opinion) to define me completely. As a consequence, I didn't really know who I was. I bounced from what I thought he wanted me to be to what she wanted. I finally became aware of just how completely codependency had taken control of my life. What anyone might have thought of me had become far more important than who I actually wanted to be.

Fortunately, people can change. We don't have to do what we always have done; after all, doing so will always produce the same result. Being selective about how we act in every situation means we will show up as the people we really are, or strive to be. And then what others think won't bother us at all. We will know we have put our best foot forward.

How we meet today and all the opportunities it presents is what defines us — nothing else.

7.

**Partial commitment to a task results in partial success.
We can make the decision to do far better than that.**

Committing one's self to whatever task compels you will take you
a long way toward completion and probable success. But where so
many fall down is the continuous effort that's required. We can't do
anything partially and expect to meet with the success we desire.
Frankly, it's all or nothing, and far too many settle for nothing.

But it's not about working from dawn to dusk every day; it's about
staying committed and doing a little at a time until the project is
complete. Every one of us can fulfill that requirement if we really
want to meet with success, one step and one day at a time. That's
what's required. And the payback is that we feel good about
ourselves when we set a goal and then go about completing it.

*Today is ripe with possibility. We can set a new goal and then take step one.
Tomorrow is step two.*

8.

**Instead of letting your hardships and failures
discourage or exhaust you, let them inspire you.
—Michelle Obama**

Failures are a fact of life. I'm reminded of the more than a thousand
failed attempts at inventing the lightbulb that Edison made. But
he didn't quit; he was inspired to keep trying by his certainty that
he was on the right track. The Wright Brothers are great examples
too, as is Madame Curie. All of them were propelled by their
determination to continue working when others thought their
endeavors were probably all for naught.

These folks didn't have anything that the rest of us don't also have.
We simply have to stay the course. We are inspired to move in a
certain direction because we have been open to the inner voice of
wisdom. We will only veer off course if we lose hope or allow others
to dissuade us from making our dreams a reality.

Staying the course, no matter what our task is today, is the only path to success. Belief in ourselves and the Voice that guides us is the way.

9.

As we express our gratitude, we must never forget that the highest form of appreciation is not to utter words, but to live by them.
— John F. Kennedy

We constantly reveal who we really are to others by our actions and our responses to the many people and situations we face every day. How we show up tells everyone all they really want to know about us. Do we take even a moment to show our appreciation when we cross paths with a friend, or better yet, with a stranger? Can we maintain our awareness that no one, absolutely no one, crosses paths with us accidentally? Let's be vigilant.

Life could be so much more meaningful and peaceful if we remembered how everything that is happening is filled with purpose. Throughout the whole day, nothing is superfluous. Every tiny detail of the day, each interaction, every smile, every rushed response plays its part in the totality of who we are to our community of onlookers. Are we going to be at peace with our own "performance" at the end of the day?

Today is the first day of the rest of our lives: an old idea, but one never more true than today. Let's be the difference that someone else needs in their life.

10.

Nothing in life is to be feared, it is only to be understood.
— Marie Curie

Our search to understand life, one another, and many other unknowns is what encourages us to get up every day. The limits of our understanding shouldn't discourage us, but should rather excite us.

Our limitations mean that our search for meaning, for greater understanding of both the lessons of the past and what may happen next, motivates us to approach and attend to the next lesson to which we are divinely led. Knowledge is the cousin of wisdom, and knowledge comes first.

Having the whole world before us, a world we understand so little of, is the most exciting aspect of being alive for many people. However, some may fear the multitude of unknowns; to them, the unknowns seem unending and overwhelming. But such mysteries call out to those who want to tackle fear and want to show the rest of us that, in the end, nothing is to be feared—nothing at all.

How exciting it is to wake up each day knowing there is something new calling to us, something we haven't encountered before. Greet what comes with enthusiasm.

11.
To make life a little better for people less fortunate than you, that's what I think a meaningful life is.
—Ruth Bader Ginsburg

Wisdom and maturity teach us that there are two things that enrich our lives and the lives of all members of the human community: being aware of the needs of others and having the compassion and willingness to take even small actions on their behalf. There are many scientists who would even say that doing *one kind thing for any living being anywhere* impacts the whole living universe. We are interconnected with all life. The influence any action has on all living things is commonly referred to as the butterfly effect.

How this translates on a daily basis is that we need not think beyond today, but it's helpful to ourselves and to all living beings to be kind, gentle, and tender in our treatment of at least one other person each day. We have no idea how our action will shape their future actions, but ask yourself, "How do I feel when someone is genuinely kind to me?" Most of us are inspired to pay a kindness forward. All kinds of things are improved as a result.

We can all add benefit to the lives of so many by just taking loving notice of the person standing before us.

12.
Nothing can stop the power of a committed and determined people to make a difference in our society.
— John Lewis

Making a difference is the calling of those who live thoughtful, intentional lives. Perhaps we aren't all called to that pursuit. And that's okay, just as along as we don't stand in the way of those who are called to make a difference. But let's consider what the value is of making a difference. First, others are positively impacted; lives may well be changed for the better for years to come. The one taking the positive action has an elevated spirit and that can have far-reaching consequences on health, both physical and mental; and spiritual well-being too.

We are not separate from any action we take. It not only emanates from us, it defines us. And we should ask ourselves, before any more time has elapsed, how do I want to be defined? What kind of a legacy do I want to leave, now and for the future? Time does not stand still. Take a moment right now to consider, "Are you being who you really want to be? Have you made a mark on the universe that you can feel proud of?"

Today awaits our involvement. Let's make sure we end the day feeling good about how we impacted those around us.

13.
The most precious gift we can offer others is our presence. When mindfulness embraces those we love, they will bloom like flowers.
— Thich Nhat Hanh

The beauty of this philosophy is that it's easily practiced by everyone of us. All that's required is a decision. We may have to remake the decision throughout the day, particularly if we have a lapse in attention. We can so easily become mindless when mindfulness is called for. But it can become a habit with disciplined practice and a desire to truly make a difference. The unexpected joy that comes to us from being fully present is our own peace of mind.

It doesn't take many tastes of peace of mind to become hungry for it on a regular basis. Having a peaceful mind allows us to ponder whatever calls to us in a quiet way. It is the constant that encourages us to act from a place of love in all our encounters. Being at peace is truly like no other state of mind and it's the only avenue to actually being able to fully embrace every person who has need of our attention. They are the ones who will always head in our direction.

Let's be ready today to fully embrace the presence of whoever God sends to us to be loved and attended to. It will be the very encounter our own journey has been waiting on.

14.

The best way to cheer yourself up is to try to cheer somebody else up.
—Mark Twain

What a simple suggestion and it carries a mighty wallop. As has been said, nothing changes if nothing changes. Everything has the potential of changing with one small, incremental change in us. Just give a smile to the first person you meet on the street, on the job, or in the grocery, and see how changed you feel inside. There really isn't anything very mysterious about cheering yourself up. All we really ever have to do is take the focus off of ourselves, and say something loving or kind to friend or stranger, alike.

The really good news about cheering someone else up is that it heightens our own peace of mind. It feels good to help someone else feel good. Our inner spaces are softened and made to smile when we make someone else smile too.

We act like life is so confusing sometimes. On the contrary, it's as simple as moving forward, one step at a time, with a smile in our hearts.

Having an assignment like cheering someone else up today is a good reason to get out of bed. Perhaps we can cheer up many people, in fact, and bless ourselves in the process.

15

Taking the time to pause before taking any action can change the trajectory of one's personal history.

Taking a deep breath to ponder options before saying or doing anything when confronted by a situation one hadn't expected can, and often does, change the outcome of whatever experience one has encountered. And yet, it's so hard to pause sometimes. It's almost more normal to react all too quickly and then find we have to undo, in the best way possible, the distress our reaction caused. But let's not fret. A habit can always be changed with willingness and determination. And taking too little time to think through the better response is just a bad habit.

There really is very little in our lives that can't be tweaked to make just a bit better. Most of us are pretty good, in most ways; however, taking the time to be a little kinder could result in a major shift in the universe. Sound too unlikely? Think again. One small kindness as the result of one tiny pause is multiplied many times over. What you and I do inspires others. Nothing happens in a vacuum.

Knowing we are a necessary part of the interconnectedness of all living beings is the exciting fact that encourages us to greet whomever wanders our way, today.

Bidden or not bidden, God is here.
—Carl Jung

The simplicity of this idea is so appealing. God simply is. He is here, now. And He always will be. Anyone of us can review our past and find evidence of the presence of God in any number of experiences. Perhaps God showed up in the nick of time when you were about to step off a curb into oncoming traffic. Or like in my case, a fateful knock at the door came just as the gas was about to be turned on ending a life. I knew God sent the visitor, a woman unknown to me. We may not be aware that God is always traveling with us. And He doesn't mind. He will stick close by anyway.

Waking up every day with the complete assurance that whether we think about God or not, He will be thinking about us is so comforting. He doesn't need us to invite Him to be present. He will be present regardless. Take a look back at your experiences in the last few days. You will no doubt see evidence of God's faithful presence, again and again. We don't have to even call on God to get His attention. It's a given.

Today you and God will live in concert. Just like was the case yesterday. And will be tomorrow.

17.

In the practice of tolerance, one's enemy is the best teacher.
—The Dalai Lama

Being tolerant is a learned skill for most of us. And it's not often learned very quickly. That we are so often in the company of people we have to be tolerant of is not accidental. They wandered our way, unknowingly, to serve as our teachers. We can decide to be grateful for them. We will become better people as a result of our willingness to tolerate them. And the greater our tolerance becomes, the fewer the people who get under our skin will become too.

We always get exactly what we need in this life to become who we are destined to be. God is always helping us out. We can be assured that each person who disrupts our peace of mind is offering us another chance to be peaceful in spite of their presence. In fact, their very presence is the gift we needed today.

Being peacefully tolerant is a given if we utilize God's ever-present help. Every person we meet up with today might be another opportunity.

18.

Do I not destroy my enemies when I make them my friends?
—Abraham Lincoln

Becoming a friend with someone is generally based on making a decision that has been borne out of clear thinking and the willingness to let differences slide by the wayside, knowing they are only as important as we have decided they are. And we can change our minds. Hallelujah. *A Course in Miracles* says the holiest place on earth is where an ancient hatred has become a present love. And I think this is clearly another way of interpreting Lincoln's question. We have it within our power to switch courses, and our perspective shifts with us.

Freedom to align ourselves with friends and strangers alike is the gift we are given every day. And no one need be an enemy, ever. We can have differing opinions, and hear one another out, but we need not turn on each other. We may not be swayed by another's opinion but wisdom and maturity allow us to appreciate the plethora of ideas that prevail in this world we share with so many. Deciding we don't have to be right is the clearest and shortest pathway to peace of mind that we will ever find.

Let's choose peace over the need to be right today.

19.

If we could change ourselves, the tendencies in the world would also change. As a man changes his own nature, so does the attitude of the world change towards him.
— Ghandi

Various versions of this well-known quote are seen on posters, on T-shirts, in greeting cards, and even on cups, and it's such a simple suggestion. There is no expectation of a massive change required of any one of us; we can just make a tiny one that reflects kindness and acceptance of others as they are. If each one of us chose to greet everyone from a place of love on any given day, nothing would remain the same in this world we share. A massive shift would occur in the universe, and all people would feel blessed.

We can be a part of that shift. There is nothing very difficult about it. It might well ask nothing more than each one of us making a pause before responding to whatever is happening in our midst. Too commonly, we act before considering how our actions will be understood by others, and then we can't take back the hurt we have caused. But there is another way to navigate through life; we can be thoughtful and constantly consider how our actions will be interpreted by others. Ask yourself, "Would I want to be on the receiving end of what I am about to say or do?"

Being a better example of ourselves isn't really all that hard. It takes willingness and persistence, both qualities we have in abundance.

20.
A great man is always willing to be little.
—Ralph Waldo Emerson

Pride prevents some people from humbling themselves enough to show up as ordinary folks. And we can all instantly recognize who those people are. Just as quickly, we gravitate toward people who aren't intent on behaving as if they are better than us, even when they have achieved great success. These individuals appreciate us for who we are, and in the process, we are inspired to see them as gracious, loving men and women.

How nice it is to simply feel like we fit in and then pay that same honor to everyone we meet in turn. Lording it over others is always a sign of an insecure, small-minded person. Great people never cast themselves as greater than anyone else. It's generally their intent to put others at ease. We can all be examples of that kind of greatness, no matter what we have or have not materially achieved in our lives.

Those we encounter today will come in all shapes and sizes. However, we will recognize in an instant who they are within.

21.
Don't count the days. Make the days count.
—Muhammad Ali

Here is a very easy recipe for making the days count: make the decision every day to do something kind for someone else and then stay mum about it. The best gifts are always those we don't gloat over. Remembering that everyone who crosses our path is on divine assignment changes how we look at each person. There are no unnecessary visitors on our path.

I think it's safe to say that everyone alive wants to feel fulfilled every day. It's probably also true that most people assume it takes doing something pretty impressive in order to feel really good. Yet, the truth is quite the opposite: the simpler our actions, the easier they are to implement, and the more likely we will then be able to take more such actions in the future. Nobody says we only have to act thoughtfully once a day. The more we take sincerely thoughtful actions, the greater number of people are being blessed by us.

Today will be rife with opportunities to toss kindnesses around like penny candy. And as every piece lands, someone smiles. How great is that?

22.
The root of suffering is attachment.
— Buddha

We all attach ourselves to people, places, and things, never considering how that is setting us up for major disappointment down the line. Many of us grew up in families that fostered unhealthy attachment. Perhaps our own insecurities pushed us to attach to a favorite friend or to someone we'd envisioned we'd partner with for life. Because we simply can't control the actions of others, attachments can be a setup for a major downfall.

What a sad state that is for the person who feels he or she must hang on to that "perfect partner" in order to survive. We can all relate and perhaps have even experienced this ourselves. The suffering can feel overwhelming. Fortunately, when we realize the way out of our suffering, even the first hint of our coming freedom will sustain our determination to make better choices.

Appreciating others is God's hope for us. Trying to possess others is not part of His plan, nor is it part of the divine journey we are here to make.

23.
Our life is frittered away by detail. Simplify, simplify.
— Henry David Thoreau

Keeping our lives simple is surely an easy path to peace of mind.
The greater the number of folks in favor of peaceful minds, the
gentler will be the journey each one of us is making, and that adds
up to a gentler world. It's not that paying attention to details is bad.
On the contrary, many professions demand it, but focusing on the
whole picture and moving toward it rather than getting lost in the
details is the real point of our lives.

Details can keep us sidetracked. While it's true we may be required
to be fastidious about work-related details: being an accountant,
an airline pilot, a cashier at the grocery all require that we pay
close attention to what we are doing, for instance; but having the
details be all of who we are is what we need to avoid if we are ever
to experience true peace in our lives. And isn't that what we are all
finally seeking?

*Being at peace, even in the midst of a very stressful job, is possible. God will
lead the way.*

24.
Someone is sitting in the shade today because someone planted a tree a long time ago.
— Warren Buffett

The beauty of interconnectedness can't be overstated. What is done
by any one of us is ultimately felt by every one of us. This is the
beautiful mystery of our lives. Wherever we go, whatever we do, we
have an impact on the lives of many, most of whom we may never
know. Yet our input makes an indelible mark on how their lives
evolve. Allowing ourselves to feel the beauty and the mystery of
how we are connected touches our lives in unforgettable ways. We
are always making a difference, somewhere, to someone.

A man like Warren Buffett has certainly touched the lives of many
people. We so often think few of us have the same power to touch

the lives of others as a wealthy magnate, but we'd be wrong to think that. Everything we do wends around the lives of men and women everywhere, and then they in turn touch many others. The circle is unending, just as the ripple on the ocean from the stone we skipped across the water reaches a shore we will never see.

Just knowing that today we will have a perfect opportunity to have a positive impact on at least one person, who will bless someone else in turn, means we are contributing to the wonderful mystery of life. And all we had to do was breathe.

25.

I don't think of all the misery but of the beauty that still remains.
—Anne Frank

Anne Frank chose to look at life from a place of love instead of fear, and it made all the difference in her short life. What she managed to do in her few short years should serve as a clear example to each of us that no one else is in charge of our mood, how we look at our experiences, or whether or not we will find peace of mind. She found it in spite of living under the constant threat of death for the last several years of her young life.

We each have the capacity to decide to live hopefully, to see the brighter side of every experience, to breathe in the powerful presence of peace each moment. And yet, we so often turn our backs on these good choices. We don't have to do what we have always done, however. We can always choose again and reap the benefit of a better decision.

Let's celebrate the knowledge that we will be as peaceful as we make up our minds to be today.

26.

Be kind whenever possible. It is always possible.
—Dalai Lama

Simple suggestions are the best kind. They are always manageable, and this particular one by the Dalai Lama is one of those. There's nothing complicated in the suggestion, nothing to sort out or even ponder over. It's reminiscent of Mother Teresa's "Be kind to everyone, and start with the person standing next to you." Let's just get on with living in the simplest way possible. There is no need to complicate any part of our lives. Just be. And do it lovingly.

Can there really be anything more inviting than knowing all we have to do on any day is express a bit of kindness? It will change the moment for everyone, especially for each one of us who is doing "the expressing." What I am suggesting here is being part of a movement to make life better for everyone. Strangers are not excluded, nor are those whom we have vehemently judged in the past. Young or old, everyone gets our offering of kindness. But it is we who are actually most blessed.

Today's assignment is simple. All we have to do is start by being kind to the first person we encounter. The rest is easy.

27.
Do what you can, with what you've got, where you are.
— Theodore Roosevelt

This is a wise suggestion, one we should take to heart because it encompasses all of us. Opportunities to make a difference in both our own lives and others' are meted out equally. We aren't expected to do great things. But doing something on behalf of humankind is great in and of itself. The fact that we all have it within our power to make a difference makes it worth getting up every morning.

Stop and consider: when was the last time you felt you made a difference in someone else's life? Then ask yourself if it was hard to do. I'm guessing everyone reading this has taken notice of someone else, clearly looked at another person, letting them know they have been seen. That's making a difference. It need not be any more complicated than that. Offering one other person rapt attention is indeed the fulfillment of God's will in the moment. And it's doing what you can where you are.

The opportunities will be many today to help someone else. We need only take one of them to make a difference.

28.
Love all, trust a few, do wrong to none.
—William Shakespeare

I thing that to live more peacefully is the goal at any age. But it has surely become my goal as I have aged. Too many years of my life were lived in turmoil. Perhaps the same is true for you. Even short-term disappointments can be exaggerated into monumental life disruptions. But they need not be. Taking each day and living it with the intention of loving others—dedicated to doing no wrong to anyone else—guarantees the day will end up feeling quite peaceful. We can all do this. And we can let the rest go by the wayside.

Perhaps we think loving everyone is more than we can commit to doing. As the Dalai Lama so famously said some years ago, "If you can't love everyone, at least don't hurt anyone." That is doable. Love may be too big of an expectation with respect to some individuals who are crossing your path, but not hurting them— doing no wrong in any way—is not beyond anyone of us. Start small; start with one person.

The rest of our lives lies before us, beginning today. May we live our lives lovingly and reap the peaceful benefits.

29.
You have power over your mind—not outside events.
Realize this, and you will find strength.
—Marcus Aurelius

None of us enjoy being told that we are not in control. Many of us tend to judge our own worth by how effectively we think we are controlling both life events and others' opinions and actions. 12-step programs like Al-Anon are replete with men and women who have spent much of their lives trying to control the alcohol and drug use of loved ones. But controlling what others choose to do will always remain outside the bounds of what's possible.

Until we fully understand how this actually is a blessing to us, we may be disheartened. But bearing full responsibility for others' behavior as well as the outcomes of all external events would truly make life burdensome. Just being in charge of ourselves is quite enough. And the sooner we understand this, the more peacefully we will experience the rest of our life.

We are saved today from being in charge of what anyone else does. We can breathe deeply and thank God.

30.

I remember the old man who said he had known a great many troubles, but most of them never happened.
—President James A. Garfield, 1881

How true this statement is in all of our lives. We worry ourselves to utter distraction about the what-ifs on our journey, but by and large, nothing that we ever worry about comes to pass and all that time has been wasted. Perhaps we could consider nurturing a mindset of positive expectation rather than always being swallowed up by doom and gloom. And just possibly we could cultivate the belief that *only what should happen on our journey will happen* — nothing more and nothing less. We can actually just sit back and wait for our lives to unfold.

This may sound foolish or even lazy to some of you, but my eight decades on this planet have taught me that nothing happens by accident. I may not have always realized just how perfect the rhythm of my life was, but hindsight has made all of what I doubted quite clear. You and I are both exactly where we are by intention. Our journeys perfectly intersect with others,' and not one of us has to worry about it.

Today can be as peaceful as anyone wants it to be. All we have to remember is that there is nothing at all to worry about; all is according to plan.

DECEMBER

1.

**To live anywhere in the world today and be
against equality because of race or color is like
living in Alaska and being against snow.
— William Faulkner**

Unfortunately, we aren't living in a society that considers all men and women equal, in spite of our Constitution and the Bill of Rights. The human rights of all people are not revered in many nations around the world. What a sad fact of life this is in the twenty-first century. What's even sadder is the possibility that people will never change. There may always be strife between segments of the population because of color, religion, ethnicity, and the list goes on.

But one by one, we can change, and we can help those around us change too. It's been my observation that people sit in judgment of others, regardless of who those others are, because they feel they have been personally treated unfairly by someone somewhere, and they want to hold somebody (or some group) responsible. If each one of us makes a pledge to ourselves (and thus to others too) that we will always act from a place of kindness and love regardless of who we encounter, worldwide change will begin to happen — one person at a time.

Today will afford us many opportunities to be an expression of love. Let's not pass them up. It's what contributes to peaceful lives.

2.

**Success? For me, success is inner peace.
— Denzel Washington**

Being peaceful is a gift that relies on choice. No one else is responsible for our peace, for initiating it nor preventing it. It rests entirely with us, moment by moment. And that's good news for all of us. A successful life is available to all of us when we define it as inner peace, because there is nothing mysterious or unattainable

EACH DAY A RENEWED BEGINNING

about inner peace. It's as close as our very next breath. We simply have to choose it.

Approaching others from a peaceful place means we will bring benefits to every encounter we have. To be recognized by others as a person who blesses every moment of life's experiences is a great honor, yet the capacity to be that person is not beyond any one of us. Being a standard-bearer for peace isn't too lofty for any of us — we need only choose it. And in the process, we will know we have mattered. What's more successful than that?

The desire for inner peace may not call to everyone, but for those who seek it out, it will be found—and every moment of one's life from that point forward will be changed forever.

3.
An active listener is to be prized above rubies.
— Ruth Humlecker

We can all usually detect whether another is listening to us or not. And of course, we all want to think that what we have to say is worth hearing. But not everyone we encounter has the capacity or the willingness to deeply hear and truly listen to what we may need to share. And when that happens, a perfect holy moment has been missed. Fortunately, we will have many opportunities every day to be active listeners and to be heard, as well.

What is so important about listening to another person? Besides the kindness and respect it demonstrates, some believe that we hear God's messages to us through the voices of others. Count me in that group of believers. God is always trying to reach us. We may read a passage in a book that strikes a perfect chord and answers the very question that was troubling us. But it is easier than that to turn our minds and ears toward all the individuals we will encounter each day. What we need to know will surface.

Nothing is wasted in a day. We meet who we need to meet. We have a chance to hear what we need to hear. And the opportunity to say what someone else needs to hear will present itself.

4.

When things change inside you, things change around you.

Many of us have wasted years of our lives thinking we'd be happy if only he/she would change, or if we had received that promotion or lived in the house of our dreams, or if it would quit raining when we have a picnic planned. We too easily place our focus outside of ourselves. We still can't ever change the external world without revamping our inner world first. But the power to see the world outside ourselves differently is as close as the decision to change our minds.

How lucky for us that in truth, we have the power to change how we see everything around us. Shifting our perspective is one decision that's capable of changing our entire day — or better yet, our entire future. Seeking inner peace is the most advantageous avenue to making that positive change, and when we look for ways to be peaceful, everything in our experience takes on a different hue. It's really not so very far to go from a troubled inner mind to one that's willing to see the light, and there is not one of us who is incapable of making this kind of change. Therefore, not one of us has to remain stuck in the old story of our lives.

Life will reflect the picture we project. No one is in charge of our own projector but ourselves.

5.

**If you don't know the guy on the other side of the world, love him anyway, because he's just like you.
— Frank Sinatra**

This is an excellent suggestion, one that is full of compassion. It is perhaps not one we might have expected from Sinatra; however, his heart was surely in the right place when he said this. We can all emulate this suggestion; not only will we be the better for it ourselves if we do, we will make the world a far better place. Tiny inroads are the easiest to make, and we don't need to initiate more than one or two positive changes a day to be the transformation we really want to see in the world.

What does it mean to love someone else? Particularly a stranger? I think it falls into the same category as being kind and tolerant. We aren't talking about romantic love but acceptance, full acceptance of the other people we encounter: *agape* or unconditional love, not *eros*. Doing that involves not holding anything back — affirming them fully with our minds and hearts. No one remains the same when we greet those around us in this way, particularly ourselves.

Loving others is the surest way to change our hearts and lives. What are we waiting for?

6.

Peace brings with it so many positive emotions that it is worth aiming for in all circumstances.
— Estella Eliot

Aiming for peace is a very interesting challenge, isn't it? We will never arrive at peace if we haven't set our minds on trying to achieve it; some would even say that "trying to achieve it" is making unnecessary work of the process. Better perhaps to just let it happen by clearing our minds of their all-too-common clutter. A peaceful mind is available to us just as soon as we decide that's what we want to experience. Our part of the bargain is to free our minds up from the cacophony that we allow to steal our attention instead of the call to be peaceful. We can make another choice as we take this very next breath.

Cultivating a peaceful mind brings inner joy, along with the desire to greet others with kindness. Engendering conflict is an option that simply doesn't occur to the one who has turned to peace. Every moment of every day left for us to live can be far better than all the moments before if we turn our minds to the gift of peace. It will never hide from us. It's always waiting to be claimed. Why not now?

Choosing peace changes not only our own life, but the lives of those we have the good fortune of encountering today. How we treat them makes a big difference to all of our lives.

---------------------- 7. ----------------------

**No person, no place, and no thing has any power over
us, for we are the only thinkers in our minds.**
—Louise L. Hay

It is so common to want to blame someone or something else for our
misfortunes. But it can be a tough pill for some to swallow when
they're reminded that we're solely responsible for our hardships
because we are in charge of what we are thinking and therefore in
charge of what our thoughts manifest on a minute-by-minute basis.
For others, though, it's good news, because it means they have an
opportunity to opt for serenity starting right now, ensuring that
their lives can change immediately.

It does become habitual to blame others for our stumbles. The
idea of taking full responsibility for them can seem unfair to the
less mature among us. It requires at least a modicum of wisdom
to willingly accept all that is our life, which means being fully
responsible for all the bad experiences along with the good. But the
sooner we understand this, the greater will be our rewards.

*No longer believing that others should be blamed for the ills of our lives is
quite freeing. Let's be aware of how this feels today.*

---------------------- 8. ----------------------

**We look forward to the time when the Power of
Love will replace the Love of Power. Then will
the world know the blessings of peace.**
—William Gladstone

Love can be a powerful influence in our lives. Love is the total
absence of judgment. It's pure acceptance, with no holding back.
And it's the inner voice reminding us that all is well and that God
is present, here and now. The overwhelming peace we feel is all the
evidence we need of God's constancy.

Expressing love to our fellow travelers certainly quiets our minds,
and we are flooded with inner peace. How much gentler our lives
would be if we dispensed with all expressions but love. We'd no

longer have to even consider what the "right" thing to say or do is in any instance. It would always be extending the hand of love.

Unfortunately, we don't yet live in a world that truly values peace. Every televised news network offers evidence of this. But we can turn away from the constant judgment that appeals to some, instead offering love to all people. By doing so, we will be sowing peace.

Today can open the door to a new way of living. Let's give expressing love a try.

9.

**Peace cannot be kept by force. It can only
be achieved by understanding.**
—Albert Einstein

Peace can be understood from many angles. There can be peace between nations, hopefully; there can be peace between members of a family who are committed to it; and there can be peace in a neighborhood, though each of these can sometimes be hard to achieve where there are many conflicting opinions present. But then there is peace as a state of mind. For peace to exist in any of the aforementioned situations, the presence of some level of inner peace is always a necessity. It's really not that hard to attain if you truly come to value it. It takes making a wise choice, a choice to let everyone—absolutely everyone who crosses your path—have whatever beliefs they choose to espouse.

We will constantly be in the company of people who believe differently than we do. That's not an accident, since we are being "schooled" every moment of our lives. The opportunity to let others be, just be, is the biggest lesson each one of us will encounter. And every time we turn away from conflict, lovingly accepting others as they are and not expecting them to live up to our expectations, we will be adding to the peace realized by all humankind.

We all have a part to play in the peace that is possible worldwide. Are we willing to do our part today?

10.

Failure is another stepping-stone to greatness.
—Oprah Winfrey

Every experience can be interpreted as a stepping-stone to greatness when viewed from a positive perspective. We are each on a trajectory to success. How long it may take us to get where we are destined to go depends on myriad events, but the journey is not accidental. Nor are our encounters; each one of them nudges us further on the next leg of the journey to our specific greatness, an accomplishment unlike that of anyone else.

No two of us will make identical journeys, of course, and that shouldn't come as a surprise. What is needed from each one of us is unique. And with the help of God, we will be able to entirely fulfill what's expected of us. In fact, it's most important that we seek God's help, because only He has the big picture—a picture that includes the journey each one of us is making. What we can know as we move along, however, is that we are being directed to the right destination and that our arrival will be at the right time. All we have to do is listen.

Getting a set of directions for the perfect journey today is what each one of us can expect. Our part is to be willing to take the first step.

11.

What seems to us as bitter trials are often blessings in disguise.
—Oscar Wilde

Your own experience has no doubt shown you the truth of Wilde's words. Hindsight is such a great teacher. The truth of our lives is that we will always be led to what we need to experience in order to become who we are destined to be. I struggled against believing this idea when initially introduced to it. Surely the alcoholic marriage wasn't necessary. And how could having had a philandering husband have been an experience I needed? And yet, both of these occurrences led me to and through the door to getting a doctorate that hadn't been on my personal life plan at all.

I gave up second-guessing. We will be led to wherever we need to be, and no matter how dire the experiences may feel, we are not alone. We have never faced anything alone. We may not have realized the constant presence of God, but He was always there. I love being reminded that God doesn't need me to be aware of Him for Him to stick around. His constancy is as certain as the setting of the sun. In the final analysis, every experience we've had or will ever have is a blessing.

Let's look forward to all the blessings destined for us today. Some may surprise us. All are perfect.

12.

We are as happy as we make up our minds to be.
—Abraham Lincoln

I'm not sure there is any way of knowing if Lincoln actually said this, but it's certainly good advice none the less. According to many spiritual teachers, happiness is a decision. And we surely have all known folks who remained happy despite encountering extremely dire circumstances. Perhaps you find yourself gravitating toward those people. Happiness is contagious, and naturally we all want more of it. The question is: are we willing to lay aside our egos long enough to see the good in all people and every situation? Unless we can say yes to this question, happiness may always elude us.

The good news is that we can make the decision to see our lives from a different perspective. We can seek out those people who are always "up" and we can follow their example. Remember, happiness is a simple decision but one that may need to be made, again and again until it replaces the old habit of always sitting on the sidelines and grumping.

Today will offer us many opportunities to be happy, rather than the alternative. It's our choice to take any one of them.

13.

**Learning to ignore things is one of the
greatest paths to inner peace.
— Saroj Singh**

There are some who might say ignoring things is simply putting your head in the sand. Anyone reasonable would have to agree that some situations should not be ignored: a call for help, for instance or a child falling down a flight of stairs. Even the incessant ringing of a cellphone can't be ignored for long. But it's all too common that we allow ourselves to be sidetracked by the unimportant, allowing all hope of inner peace to escape us.

The solution is learning to be alert to those things that are important so we can let the rest slip by. Being selective about what we allow to capture our attention is the most obvious way to stay on the path to realizing inner peace. Serenity is always available to us. We just have to want it enough to stay focused on its attainment.

Each day is offering many opportunities for distraction. But just as many opportunities for inner peace are available. Which we choose is up to us.

14.

**The best way to make your dreams come true is to wake up.
— Paul Valéry**

This quote may make us smile, but it's also right on the mark. To accomplish anything at all, we must first greet the day. Then next on the agenda is making an intention for what one hopes to achieve. Every person reading this has no doubt had their dreams foiled. But we have all met with success too on even more occasions. It's good to remember that not every dream is really one that's meant to materialize, at least not at the time it is attempted. There is a right time for everything that happens in our lives.

It's not always easy to remember that God is in charge of the timing of the events in our lives, but hindsight will reveal how true this is. We will meet who we need to meet at the perfect time. We will always be in the right place at the right time for the next experience that's intended for our growth. If this idea seems farfetched, reflect for a bit. You are here now, reading this, because of your specific journey. Your dream, whether you realize it or not, is coming true.

All is happening on time. And all is well. These are truths we can take to the bank.

15.
No way exists in the present to accurately determine the future effect of the least of our actions.
— Gerald Jampolsky

This quote reminds us that every action taken by any one of us is part of a thread, not only of all of our actions, but of all actions taken by anyone. Scientists believe our interconnectedness is irrefutable. Many also believe that our connections to others includes not just humans, but *all living things*. That is worth factoring into our behavior, since we humans often carelessly disregard other life-forms. We need each other, one and all.

Looking at all actions and interactions from this perspective ought to make us far more respectful of this planet we share with trillions of life-forms. Let's not forget the theory of the butterfly effect, which stipulates that even a tiny change in one life form will be transmitted to another and then another and on to infinity. In other words, the impact of what you or I do here and now has no finite ending. Let's remain thoughtful.

Let's not be careless in our actions today. What we do has a very long reach.

16.
Things that happen aren't necessarily good or bad; they just fit into my plans, or they don't.
— Anne Arthur

We are so good at making plans. Unfortunately, we frequently forget that God has His own time table for the experiences He wants us to have. And the truth is that every experience is meant for our good, even when it may feel bad to us initially. Hindsight has so much to teach us. Everyone reading this was absolutely sure that some experience in his/her past was disastrous, only to discover in the next week or month or year that it was perfect to the tee.

We simply don't see the whole picture of how our life will unfold in any one moment. Certainly no individual experience is more than a sliver of the whole of our lives. The plans that you and I make, though oftentimes complimentary to those plans that God has in store for us, have to be adjusted to fit the bigger puzzle of our life. God will make the adjustment. Our assignment is to graciously accept that adjustment.

Today may offer us opportunities that we had no expectation of ever happening. Let's trust them to be God's small gifts to us.

17.
We do not always like what is good for us in this world.
—Eleanor Roosevelt

Without a doubt, everyone reading this brief statement can point to numerous experiences that you did not like while they had you in their grip. For sure, I can point to hundreds of them. Yet every one of them actually opened the door to a more perfect experience, one that I had no idea was on the horizon. What I have come to cherish is that our journey is always moving toward the destination that is perfect for us. As has been said before, we will arrive where we need to be and our lessons will be presented to us within our experiences along the way.

Is it irrelevant that we may not always like our experiences? Not at all, but our liking them has little to do with whether or not they are part of the journey that we agreed to before our first step was even taken. Let's remember, we are always where we need to be, experiencing people and situations that are bringing about a more perfect evolution of who we are becoming. Our lives are always in good hands. We can be grateful.

Today we will greet the next few perfect experiences in the evolutionary cycle of our lives.

18.

**We are not permitted to choose the frame of our
destiny. But what we put into it is ours.
— Dag Hammarskjöld**

Being reminded of our responsibility for all that we choose to do,
plan, think, and say helps us moment by moment as we barrel
through life. It's all too easy to make choices without thinking
things through to the end stage of each choice. However, when
we do pause, we are often prevented from doing something
we wouldn't have been proud of a bit later in the day. There is
nothing more helpful, or even powerful, some might say, than the
momentary pause. It has without a doubt saved relationships. It
might also stop wars if a well-timed pause is considered an option
before the first strike is made.

Even though our journey through life may be predetermined, there
are many potentially enlightening side trips and detours along
the way. Each one offers a lesson that we will have the privilege
of sharing with others, making their lives more meaningful in the
process. Nothing is ever wasted — nothing. What good news that is
for all of us.

*We are moving forward as God's plan dictates, but we will have many
opportunities to tarry along the way. Let's not forget that each little side trip
is of key importance too.*

19.

**Politeness is the art of choosing among one's real thoughts.
— Abel Stevens**

We all have many thoughts that would no doubt cause us to be
embarrassed if others could glimpse them. Fortunately, we have the
constant capacity to select those we think are worthy to be heard
by all of our fellow travelers. On occasion, we let slip a thought or
two that we can't take back — but wish we could. That happens to
all of us, but we do get better with practice. When we utilize the all-
powerful pause before giving voice to anything, we generally sound
far wiser and certainly far kinder too.

Choosing to be polite might not be a quality we have valued. But probably we have all taken notice of people around us who are polite, even (or particularly) in difficult circumstances. Their behavior stands out, and many of us long to be able to emulate them. There is no mystery about emulating them, though; it's all about asking a simple question: who do I really want to be? Make a choice and then follow through.

Choosing to be polite all day long is a worthy choice. The more of us who make it, the more peace there will be throughout the world.

20.

Peace comes from being able to contribute the best that we have, and all that we are, toward creating a world that supports everyone.
—Hafsat Abiola

Peace is an interesting concept, one with many aspects. There is peace between nations, a worthy goal, although one not always easily attained between factions that have been at loggerheads for decades. Perhaps some nations will never be at peace with their neighbors. And then there is peace, or the lack of it, within communities, particularly communities where many cultures are represented. Protecting one's turf can become all-important in those neighborhoods. Peace within our families is closest to home and perhaps concerns us the most. Not seeing eye-to-eye with blood relatives can be the most painful disharmony of all.

But in all of these situations there is a solution, one that fits snugly in every circumstance. Becoming willing to see every situation from the perspective of the other person takes the sting out of the differences that previously crippled communication. In every instance, being willing to step back and seek the inner quiet and the peaceful guidance of the God of one's understanding will change how the circumstance appears.

Being willing to give peace a chance is all that's ever required when disagreement has torn people apart. This isn't beyond anyone.

21.
Act as if what you do makes a difference. It does.
— William James

For some, it's jarring to learn that everything they do counts and even makes a difference. Nothing that is said or done is without effect. This can be unsettling, for sure. But it's also a great opportunity to be mindful of all that we are thinking and doing. There are those who believe our thoughts, not unlike our actions, can manifest in either positive or negative ways; they are vibrational, which means they are constantly impacting the planet.

It's really quite fortuitous that nothing that is said or done is wasted. It allows each one of us to make both small and large differences throughout our lives. If given even a moment to reflect on it, nary a one of us wants to have a negative impact on the world. When we know we are making a difference just by the very nature of being alive and making choices, it is a big responsibility. It's also a real gift to us and to all of those we will touch, providing our actions are kind and loving.

Today is a blank canvas, open for our involvement. Let's make it loving and helpful, over and over.

22.
Peace is never more than a decision away.

Why is it that we allow so many moments of our lives to be wasted in agitation, or worse? There is nothing all that mysterious about choosing to be peaceful. It's no bigger a decision than brushing our teeth or smiling at a child at the grocery. We simply have to want it, and frankly, most would agree that there is nothing better than the times when we are quiet and free from angst or upset of any kind. They soothe us, and we all deserve to be soothed.

We can decide that peace, living it and fostering it in others, will be a priority. The living of it comes first, of course. And utilizing the proverbial pause before saying or doing anything brings us one step closer to being a proponent of peace. We can't take back words — or actions. We can make amends, but we'd never have to do that if we took a moment to be "with ourselves" each time before we said something we might regret or acted in a way we'd be ashamed of. Our lives can be completely different than they are now—if we want them to be.

How exciting to know that what lies before us today is uncharted territory. Let's make the day one we will be proud of at day's end.

23.
When people bother you in any way, it is because their souls are trying to get your divine attention and blessing.
—Catherine Ponder

This may well be a refreshing new way of looking at the folks who drive us to distraction. For many of us, myself included, it is so important to reframe how we look at the people who travel by our sides. It's not uncommon for our first thought to be a critical one. It's so easy to be judgmental. Unfortunately, for far too many of us, it's our first response.

But we can change, particularly when we are offered a whole new way of looking at our fellow travelers. Every one of them is seeking our blessing, whether they are "bothering" us or not. Making the decision to look at every person we meet from this perspective changes our outlook completely. But more than that, it changes the interactions, and that in turn has the power to change all of our lives. How we treat any one person ripples through the entire human community. Never forget that.

Every person who crosses our path today is seeking the same thing: our blessing. Let's be generous.

24.
I will be attentive to all the signs from God today.
Whatever answer I seek is finding its way to me.
—Patrick Atchley

Believing that our answers seek us out allows us to accept the moments of uncertainty with greater ease. We will always find out what we need to know. Putting worry aside, once and for all, allows for such inner joy. And that's God's constant gift to us. He will always guide us in the best way to think, act, and respond. Our part of the "bargain" is to simply wait for the information we need to move forward. God will never fail to guide us in the right direction.

What relief this idea offers us if we take it to heart. And why wouldn't we? The demanding ego that tends to haunt us is the primary reason we turn away from God's clear guidance. Our impatience is often the real culprit. We want messages from God to show up on demand, rather than accepting that they will always come when we are truly ready for them. Choosing to be quiet and trusting while we wait would not only do us good, it would add to the peaceful vibration of the planet.

God will no doubt be trying to get our attention today. Let's be open and curious and patient.

25.

Strangely, it was comforting to me when I read that squirrels forget where they hide about half of their nuts.
— Ruth Casey

How much we are like all the other living creatures. Being imperfect is par for the course of life. The beauty of coming to appreciate our imperfections is that it allows us to be far more accepting of everyone else's as well. We are told that God isn't expecting perfection and that His love for us is certain, regardless of our failures. God doesn't even take notice of them, in fact. But we continue to focus on the faults, both in ourselves and even more in others. It's surely time for us to adopt the idea of acceptance, accepting each of us as we present ourselves in every moment.

Can you imagine how much more pleasant life would be if we simply let others be as they are and loved them fully with no critiquing at all? Not only would we feel greater peace, but we'd nurture peace in others too. We can all sense the vibe of acceptance, and likewise, we all too quickly detect the judgments others are holding against us. It's time to put all of these negative opinions of others behind us and relish all that we are here to give one another.

Life is far too short to live in a constant state of disappointment. We have what we need, and we will meet whomever is on our "schedule" today, imperfections and all.

26.
Success is not final, failure is not fatal; it is the courage to continue that counts.
—George F. Tilton

We are always in process. And what a good feeling that is. Every experience is, in actuality, an introduction to the very next perfect experience that God has selected for us. We need not fear any one of them. We will be able to handle whatever comes our way because only that which should come our way, will. We may not handle it successfully initially. And that doesn't matter in the big picture of our lives. We will always get another chance to handle something similar. What we need, we are guaranteed to receive.

This makes life pretty easily navigable. We have no reason to ever live in fear. Knowing that there is a perfect trajectory for each one of us eases our journey and our minds. There is no reason to live anxiously any more. Peaceful days will be as plentiful as is our choice to claim them. To know that we will be as peaceful as we make up our minds to be allows us to be courageous as we move forward.

Choosing courage today makes every step of our journey easier, which in turn, means that we will be good way showers for the others who travel close by.

27.
I believe that every single event in our life happens as an opportunity to choose love over fear.
—Oprah Winfrey

The choice is so clear: being loving empowers our lives, while giving in to fear imprisons us. Winfrey's statement encourages us to look at every experience that presents itself, whether it involves a friend or a total stranger, as an invitation to be loving. Unfortunately, for some, fear becomes the default state of mind. The good news is that we can cultivate another way of experiencing the events in our lives.

Every action any of us makes comes from either a place of love or a place of fear. When we understand this, it helps us make the choice to be loving in all of the encounters we experience. Being loving is as simple as being kind. It might not be anything more than a smile or an offer to be of help. It really doesn't have any romantic overtones. It's a more basic expression than that. It's a simple choice, but it is one that makes a huge difference in who we are becoming day by day.

As we have heard so many times before, today is the first day of the rest of our lives. We can make it one to cherish. The choice is not hard.

28.
Stillness is where creativity and solutions to problems are found. —Eckhart Tolle

Stillness is rich beyond belief. Besides creativity and solutions, peace of mind awaits us in the stillness. God waits there too. Stillness truly is a gift quite beyond our wildest expectations. It relieves us and renews us. It provides the calm that we seek so that we can hear God's messages. And it never fails to comfort us, whether for a moment or a day. The deep calm of even a moment of quiet can nurture peace in us throughout the day.

Never underestimate the power of stillness; simply seek it, and everything in life will undergo a quiet change. We can sustain that change by our willingness to claim a few moments of tranquility throughout every day. Its power really can't be measured, but it can be felt. Best of all, anytime anyone claims a moment of stillness, every living thing benefits.

Let's be willing to choose a few moments of stillness today. Take note of what it does for your sense of clarity and peace of mind.

29.
When I trust, any fear I had immediately dissolves.
— Ellie Atchley

It may feel like a major shift in perspective to trust that all is always in God's hands and is thus destined to turn out for the best for each of us. Many of us have no doubt assumed for far too long that we were in charge and fully responsible for the outcome of everything in our lives, and perhaps even the lives of others too. (I know I did.) It can initially be hard to fathom when we learn this is not the case. We need time to absorb such a change in our worldview. It's just not that easy to go from no trust at all to full trust in the idea that there is a power greater than we are and that He will take the reins in all instances—that He has in fact been on duty all the time.

Our lives feel so much easier when we finally turn that corner—yet we resist. How difficult we make our lives, and it is all so needless. We resist because we hate giving up the control we thought we had. We didn't actually mastermind anything. If something turned out the way we'd been angling for it to, it was only because it satisfied God as well.

Today will be full of opportunities to deliberately let God be in charge. The trade-off is that we can rest peacefully all day long, knowing we are in good hands.

30.
We have been promised that we'll arrive at our proper destination if we do the footwork and let God do the navigating.
— T.B. Kirk

We work in concert with God. We sometimes forget this; however, God does not. That is something for which we can be grateful. We are a team, and we mortals don't even have to remember that for it to effectively work on our behalf. God is completely present in our lives, from the tiniest of our endeavors to the really big challenges that we think will defeat us. As this year comes to an end, we can briefly review the many unexpected successes we experienced. We can chalk up those successes to God's helpful hand in every instance.

We are simply lucky beyond words, aren't we? It behooves us to be grateful and to help others see how perfectly their lives have unfolded too. We surely can end up making detours in our lives, and many of us have recollections of some dire ones. But we always got back on track. Why? Because God never veered from our side. No detour was too big for Him to navigate. And now, here we are, safely arriving at our destination as was expected; taking it one day at a time. God is good. Peace is ours.

Let's never forget how we got here. Let's also never forget that God has never lost sight of us, not even in our darkest hours. We simply can't shake His presence. It's a given. And so is our peace of mind.

31.
Peace begins with me. And you.

Taking charge of how we greet each moment today is the best way of ensuring our own peace of mind. It's also the surest way of encouraging a peaceful encounter with whomever God has sent our way on this day. As I have already established in other meditations, we have never and will never encounter any accidental visitors along our path. Each has come bidden to share in the lesson we both need to move on to our next challenge.

We have been carefully watched over throughout our journey. We have met who we needed to meet. We have experienced the lessons that were perfect for our particular trajectory in this life. Every door that has opened did so at exactly the right time, and those we might have reached too soon opened when the time was right. We have not traveled alone. Even when we didn't feel the Holy Presence of God, it was there. This will never change, never ever for any of us.

We can peacefully rest today knowing that our journey is in safe hands for all time. Amen.

CLOSING THOUGHTS

I always feel a mix of relief and sadness when I come to the close of a book; relief that the God of my understanding and I had the good fortune and willingness to spend a few hours away together every day making this book a possibility but a hint of sadness that our "work" for now is done. I don't mean to imply that our relationship is done. That can never be the case, but the focus of our relationship, which is my very sustenance, will be elsewhere for a time.

A word about one's relationship with God: we each have one. We may not always remember that or honor it, but God will never, ever leave our side, regardless of anything we do. In fact, as a very long-time and committed *Course in Miracles* student, I know that God and I are One. Therefore, He can't leave my side — or yours either. End of story. And I daresay, as I wrote in multiple meditations throughout this book, that this is an irrefutable fact of our spiritual existence. Aren't we lucky this is so? We can never do anything that will result in God leaving our side — never ever.

I didn't always embrace this idea. There was a time in my life that the idea of God didn't even cross my mind. It's hard to believe that now, actually, because I feel so comforted by my awareness of God's presence. I can't say it is constant, but I know where to turn when I have even a moment's doubt — about anything. What's even better is that God has not one doubt about anything.

I do hope all of you who chose to read this book are comforted by it. That was its clear intention. Finding peace on our journey, one day at a time, is the very best gift any one of us can ever hope to receive. And as I have aged, I have grown to value it even more.

I sincerely want to thank you for joining me once again in the pages of another book. Many of us have wandered this path before. Any of you who might be new to my work can look me up on Amazon for additional titles. Perhaps another book of mine from an earlier time will call to you now. I am just glad you found me on this go-round. I love knowing, as I am writing these daily thoughts, that I will be reaching new hearts, as well as touching base again with old friends.

Again, thank you, from the bottom of my heart. This quarantine turned out to be far different for me than I had first anticipated. Writing has been my salvation before. It has been doubly so over these last few months. Please let me hear from you in the weeks and months ahead. I assure you I am never more than an email away.

Love to each and every one of you.

— KAREN CASEY

karencasey@me.com
jcasey4991@aol.com
www.womens-spirituality.com
https://www.facebook.com/EDANBbyKC/

ABOUT THE AUTHOR

Karen Casey has sold over three million books that draw upon meditations, motivations, and religion to guide and support women throughout the world. Based in Minneapolis since 1964, Casey is an elementary school teacher turned PhD. Casey published the first of twenty-eight books, *Each Day a New Beginning: Daily Meditations for Women*, with Hazelden Publishing in 1982. Casey has spoken to tens of thousands worldwide over her forty years as a writer. Through each new experience, her gratitude and commitment grow to continue doing what brings joy to her life.

Additional notable works from Karen Casey include *52 Ways to Live the Course in Miracles: Cultivate a Simpler, Slower, More Love-Filled Life, Let Go Now: Embrace Detachment as a Path to Freedom,* and *A Life of My Own: Meditations on Hope and Acceptance.*

Mango Publishing, established in 2014, publishes an eclectic list of books by diverse authors—both new and established voices—on topics ranging from business, personal growth, women's empowerment, LGBTQ studies, health, and spirituality to history, popular culture, time management, decluttering, lifestyle, mental wellness, aging, and sustainable living. We were recently named 2019 *and* 2020's #1 fastest growing independent publisher by *Publishers Weekly.* Our success is driven by our main goal, which is to publish high quality books that will entertain readers as well as make a positive difference in their lives.

Our readers are our most important resource; we value your input, suggestions, and ideas. We'd love to hear from you—after all, we are publishing books for you!

Please stay in touch with us and follow us at:

Facebook: Mango Publishing
Twitter: @MangoPublishing
Instagram: @MangoPublishing
LinkedIn: Mango Publishing
Pinterest: Mango Publishing
Newsletter: mangopublishinggroup.com/newsletter

Join us on Mango's journey to reinvent publishing, one book at a time.

CPSIA information can be obtained
at www.ICGtesting.com
Printed in the USA
JSHW041903220421
13778JS00005B/5

9 781642 505665